THOUGHT TOOLS
Volume 2

THOUGHT TOOLS
Volume 2

Fifty Timeless Truths to Uplift and Inspire

_____

Rabbi Daniel & Susan Lapin

Lifecodex Publishing Company

Published by Lifecodex Publishing, LLC.,
Mercer Island, Washington.

Library of Congress Control Number: 2008940402

ISBN 978-0-9822018-1-7

Printed in the United States of America

CONTENTS

INTRODUCTION

When we began writing our weekly Thought Tools in January, 2008, we had no way of knowing what a highlight of our week it would become. Sent initially to just over 2,000 readers, we now have over ten times that number of subscribers, with many new people signing up each day. The gracious emails and notes we receive letting us know how Thought Tools has impacted lives, gratifies and encourages us.

It is quite thrilling for us to be presenting this collection of Thought Tools published online between January, 2009 and December, 2009. We feel that the introduction to *Thought Tools 2008: Fifty Timeless Truths to Uplift and Inspire* is still the best explanation for the idea behind these teachings. With a few changes, we are presenting it once again.

Some years ago, we sailed our forty-four foot sailboat, Paragon, from Los Angeles to Hawaii. From the time the California coastline dropped away behind us until we reached Diamond Head, Honolulu, twenty two days later, we were surrounded by more water than we had ever imagined. We had seen the charts, of course, and knew that the earth was mostly water, but sailing along seeing absolutely nothing but sky and ocean was an entirely different reality.

In ancient Jewish wisdom, water is seen as a metaphor for knowledge. The source of all wisdom is God's word, the Bible, or as we call it, the Torah. We were both privileged to receive a Torah education growing up, and since we found each other, an important piece of our partnership in life has been immersing ourselves in the waters of Torah and sharing what we could with others. It is deeper, broader and more enchanting than even the Pacific Ocean.

People all tend to experience physical stimuli in basically the same way. Those of us who enjoy a barbecued steak all tend to react to it in a similar manner and we all share enjoyment of a drink of cool water on a hot day. However, we react to emotions in ways a little more reflective of our own uniqueness. How one person reacts to a happy event or a sad scene might be entirely different from how his friend reacted to the very same occurrence.

Still more individual are the thoughts we each bring to life in our souls and minds. It is those thoughts that we hope to stimulate through this book and thus help bring out your own special uniqueness. We truly are what we think and what we talk about helps determine our thoughts. Just as exercise can be done correctly or incorrectly, so the time we invest in speaking and thinking can be used more or less effectively.

It is very easy to speak about people. More than that, it is also very enjoyable to speak about other people. There would hardly be so many magazines devoted to celebrity gossip were this not so. Yet there is something unappealing and unfulfilling about trying to seek content in our lives by scurrying around in the detritus of other folks' lives.

It is a little harder to speak about things though it is certainly more beneficial than speaking about other people. Some individuals can speak incessantly of places they have visited or food they have enjoyed. Others of items they have or hope to buy. This is definitely a step up, but it still leaves our souls thirsting.

Of all conversation, none does so much good and produces such creative thought as conversation about ideas. We hope these Thought Tools spur you to a greater appreciation of God's word and His world and that in sharing them with your family and friends they serve to help you grow individually and together.

How could we not thank our children? Without them, their company and their conversation, many of these ideas and insights would never have emerged. Max and Rebecca lead their family and their community with courage and love. Yoni and Rena offer a model haven of tranquility and faith. Zev and Rachelle are an incandescent beacon of warmth and generosity. Ari is a rare combination of wisdom, competence and humility. Asher and Ruthie inspire others as they live their dream. Miriam is an unstoppable phenomenon of grace, charisma, and charm. Tamara is a fortress of inner strength filled with beauty and promise. We love you and endlessly appreciate all you have done for us.

Do make sure you sign up for your free weekly Thought Tools at www.rabbidaniellapin.com. We look forward to learning and growing together.

Rabbi Daniel and Susan Lapin
January 2010   Shvat 5770

1

CAMEL POWER

Someone who automatically disagrees with popular opinion is a grouch. Someone who always agrees with popular opinion is a fool.

Go ahead and write down three of your most strongly held views in politics, culture or economics. Now be honest – how many of them did you arrive at after thorough investigation and independent analysis? The amazing truth is that we base many of our views on positions held by our friends, family or the news and entertainment media.

In 1953, psychologist Solomon Asch invited volunteers to participate in a 'scientific experiment.' They were conducted into a room with other people purporting to have responded to the same advertisement. Really, they were Solomon Asch's secret collaborators.

Asch showed drawings of various lines and asked everyone to estimate their length. When the collaborators responded accurately, so did the genuine subject. When all the collaborators responded with a prearranged wrong answer, the volunteer usually ended up agreeing with their wildly improbable figure.

The experiment was repeated in a wide variety of scenarios but the incontrovertible conclusion emerged. Most people are significantly swayed in their beliefs by what others around them think, no matter how preposterous the thinking.

This can harm our lives if we buy into untrue but popular mindsets regarding our finances, our families and our faith.

Ancient Jewish wisdom addresses this issue through a peculiar pattern in the Torah. Wouldn't you expect the Hebrew word for camel to appear fairly randomly throughout Genesis? After all, it was the main mode of transport and nearly everyone in Genesis travelled. This is how the word camel looks in Hebrew:

גמל

It turns out that over 70% of the instances of camel appearances in the entire Five Books of Moses occur in the context of the life of Isaac. Here is the first time the Hebrew word for camel, GaMaL, intersects with the life of Isaac:

> *And the lad grew and became a camel, and Abraham*
> *made a big feast on the day that Isaac became a camel.*
>
> (Genesis 21:8)

Okay, calm down. I know that your English translation reads, "And the lad grew and was weaned; and Abraham made a big feast on the day that Isaac was weaned," but I am giving you the accurate translation of the Hebrew. You can see for yourself that the root of the word I am reproducing here, which is used in verse 8, looks exactly like the word for camel that I showed you above:

גמל

Deeper meaning is often embedded in the Torah by certain words consistently conveying certain themes. What is the thematic meaning of the camel? The camel is an independent creature that can cross vast distances of dry desert. Its independence comes from consuming voluminous quantities of water.

The thematic meaning of water throughout the Torah, in addition to its literal meaning, is the entire body of Divine wisdom. This is why many languages employ the figure of speech, "thirst for knowledge."

Abraham was intent that his son, the first born Jew, should possess the advantage of spiritual and intellectual independence. Isaac needed to forge his own relationship with God, not simply believe what his father told him. Once he was filled with water (or wisdom) he would be able to traverse distances through alien territory (ideas) just like a camel. When this was achieved, Abraham made a feast.

The story about finding Isaac's bride, Rebecca, (Genesis 24:10-67) is filled with camels. Abraham's servant, Eliezer, revealed new ideas of God and Truth to Rebecca. When she decided that she must leave her family and embark on her own spiritually independent path, she naturally got up on a camel. Upon meeting Isaac, she can now share her life partner's camel so to speak. Accordingly, the camel references culminate with her getting down off her own camel in Genesis 24:64.

Someone who automatically disagrees with popular opinion is a grouch. Someone who always agrees with popular opinion is a fool. Don't leave home without your camel.

LIFE HAPPENS – NOT

**In life, things do not usually depend
on a roll of the dice.**

In malls from San Antonio to Santa Monica expensive retailers like Neiman Marcus, Tiffany and Bloomingdale's are opening new stores. That suggests many customers with money to spend, yet we all know legions of debt-strapped people struggling to keep their noses above water.

Looking at the economy, it is easy to see that some people are better off than others. However, inequality can be found in other areas too. Studying health, for instance, would reveal that some people enjoy healthier lives than others.

Now if we analyzed marriage and family trends, we would discover that some people have more successful marriages and better functioning families than others.

Some people even win what I call 'the ovarian lottery' with genes from their parents that bequeath them good looks.

Life would seem extremely unfair if all rich people were good looking, enjoyed great health and had fantastic families. However, you don't need to be a social scientist to know that this is not the case. In other words, every single human being carries his or her own bag of problems.

There may be people who seem to have it all just as there seem to be a few who are singularly cursed, but in reality all of us have blessings that call for rejoicing and challenges that call for struggle.

The wonder of being a human being is that today's woes are not tomorrow's destiny. Likewise riding high today is no guarantee that tomorrow will be all smiles. Life seems like a cosmic version of the children's board game, *Chutes and Ladders*.

Except that in life things do not depend on a roll of the dice. Most things don't just happen. You can usually track them to decisions you make, even if you fail to recognize the importance of the moment.

In countless unexpected moments, veiled opportunities that will change your destiny (for better or worse) are hiding in plain sight. It might be an instant when you either choose to step forward and fearlessly assume responsibility or you let the occasion pass. It might be the smile and courtesy you extend to someone in need witnessed by a third party who turns out to be vital to your future.

In a military encounter from Biblical times we see how big results rest on seemingly trivial decisions. In Chapter 7 of the book of Judges, God picks Gideon to rescue Israel from the Midianites. After Gideon raises an army of 32,000 men, God directs him to reduce the number so that all will recognize the forthcoming deliverance as miraculous rather than a natural victory of superior force.

When the army is down to 10,000 men, God provides Gideon with a method of further reducing it. He is directed to take the remaining soldiers down to the water and watch as they drink. While the majority of the thirsty men dip their heads into the water, 300 men use their hands to scoop water up to their mouths. That small but fateful decision draws God's favor onto them.

Ancient Jewish wisdom explains that eating is an activity we share with the animal world. For that reason, we constantly need to highlight ways of eating that demonstrate the triumph of spiritual awareness over physical desire. Lowering your head to the food or drink lowers the spiritual to the physical. Raising food or water to your head elevates the physical to the spiritual.

Stressful periods, and certainly wartime, present a particular challenge to humans. Retaining our uniquely Godly qualities demands constant effort. The men chosen to champion God against the Midianites made the small but important decision to elevate the way they drank; changing their destinies through that one action.

Understanding passages such as this one offers direction for us today to elevate our own behavior and attract God's favor.

3

FASTEN YOUR (BIBLE) BELTS

Why was the Bible given
in the desert?

Why am I convinced that economic improvement is possible in the United States and certain other countries while I am equally convinced that it is impossible in many other societies?

In typical rabbinic fashion, I shall answer that question with another question: Why did God convey His message to mankind from a remote mountain in one of the loneliest deserts in the world?

Wouldn't it have made more sense for God to have brought the Israelites to the Land of Canaan and then given them the Torah from, say, Mount Moriah in Jerusalem?

What does today's economy have to do with the Bible having been given in the desert? Well, remember this:

The Bible not only shaped the stained glass windows of Europe's greatest cathedrals, it also reverberates in the speeches of hundreds of great American leaders from John Winthrop to Ronald Reagan.

President Abraham Lincoln called the Bible, "the best gift God has given to man." This view that the Bible shaped America almost as much as it did Israel is what enabled him to say to the New Jersey Senate in 1861, "The Americans are God's almost-chosen people."

Let's glance at a few practical consequences of just three Biblical verses:

Example 1:

> *If there be a poor person, from one of your people*
> *in one of your cities in your land which the Lord*
> *your God has given you, do not harden your heart*
> *or close your hand from your poor brother.*
> *For open your hand to him, and lend to him*
> *what he is missing, whatever is lacking to him.*
> (Deuteronomy 15:7-8)

This concept of sharing in one another's misfortunes formed a social network of mutual aid and led naturally to the concept of insurance, first found in Judeo-Christian countries.

Example 2:

> *And Abram was very rich with livestock, silver and gold.*
> (Genesis 13:2.)

These words are not written as a moral indictment of Abraham, but instead convey both the idea of property rights and the moral legitimization of wealth and success, two indispensable features that make the creation of wealth possible.

Example 3:

*Observe and hear all these words which I command
you, that it may go well with you and with
your children after you forever when you do
that which is good and right in the sight
of the Lord your God.*

(Deuteronomy 12:28)

A widely shared moral code encourages behavioral consistency, which allows for stability and a sense of security. Unlike how people live day-to-day in unpredictable and fear-ridden societies, this powerful idea makes it logical to build for the long-term future

These three factors among others enabled a rag tag band of former slaves to create the nation of Israel which continues to thrive amidst peril and threat until the present day.

These three factors among others enabled a rag tag band of religious refugees to land on the shores of a vast and threatening land and create history's greatest engine of freedom and prosperity.

Earlier I asked what the Bible having been given in the desert has to do with the economy. Well, ancient Jewish wisdom teaches that had it been given in the city of Jerusalem or any other stable and populated center, we might never have learned of its transformative powers for groups as well as individuals.

Having been given to a band of refugees in the desert, we can see that it alone was responsible for them becoming a lasting and powerful nation. Similarly, early Americans crossed an ocean bringing little with them other than the Bible and its practical and transformative powers.

Included in these Biblical concepts are strong social cohesion and shared risk, protection of the rights of ownership, admiration for what I call Ethical Capitalism® and widespread commitment to social predictability through God's rule of law.

Every individual has the opportunity to promote these principles. And to the extent that enough of us successfully regenerate them, economic storms may occur and be turbulent, but they will also pass.

4

WON'T YOU BE MY FRIEND?

**Friendship depends on actions
in the same way that dance
depends upon movement.**

For the first time in the eight hundred year history of the English language, the word "friend" can be a verb. On the popular social networking site, Facebook, you can "friend" someone you barely know.

Parents delight in seeing their child proudly pointing to another kid and announcing, "That's my friend." Identifying someone as a friend is a major step in conceptual thinking for a child. Come to think of it, understanding friendship is worthwhile even for adults – maybe especially for adults – perhaps especially for adults during challenging times.

Let's examine three types of human relationships:

Mother and father are easy relationships to understand. You arrive in the world and there they are. Brother and sister are also simple. You don't have to do anything to have a brother or sister. They are presented to you and whether or not you actually like them, they always remain your siblings.

The husband and wife relationship is a little more complicated. This incredibly close and powerful relationship comes into being through a particular, deliberate and public action we call marriage. Furthermore, the Biblical Blueprint allows for its dissolution as a rare and tragic circumstance. This too requires a particular, deliberate and public action that we call divorce.

This brings us to the relationship we know as friendship. Friendship can be close and powerful but it is seldom formed by any one deliberate and public action. It usually forms gradually and when it ends, it often fades away.

This third relationship is the most mysterious of all. Unlike parent or sibling relationships, friendship is not biological. Unlike marriage, no legal process launches it. How do we form friendships and how do we preserve them?

The Lord's language, Hebrew, grants us a clue from the three distinctly different words for friend.

1. ReAH is related to "shepherd" and is found several times in the last of the Ten Commandments:

> *Don't bear false witness against your friend.*
> *Don't covet the house of your friend.*
> (Exodus 20:13 -14)

2. YeDiD is related to "hand" and is found only once in the Five Books of Moses.

> *And to Benjamin he said, 'A friend of the Lord*
> *will live in security...'*
> (Deuteronomy 33:12)

3. ChaVeR is related to "obligation" as well as being part of a unified group. Here is an example of its usage:

For if they fall, the one will lift up his _friend_...
(Ecclesiastes 4:10)

In what ways do these words differ?

The answer is that Facebook's language is actually teaching us a fundamental truth. Friend IS a verb. In other words, a friend is what you get when you do certain things. The three Hebrew words for friend point to this reality.

The first one, ReAH, is someone whose welfare is your concern, as a sheep's welfare is the concern of the shepherd. You help him by doing those things that benefit him and you avoid actions that harm him.

The second word, YeDiD, expresses symmetry. While I discuss this in detail in my popular book, *Buried Treasure – Secrets for Living from the Lord's Language*, YeDiD represents a give and take relationship. The word comprises the two-letter Hebrew word for hand repeated, like this – hand-hand, YaD-YaD

יד

Hand

ידיד

Friend

Finally, the third Hebrew word for friend, CHaVeR, is derived from the Hebrew word for obligation or indebtedness – CHoV.

An important part of friendship is helping each other thus making a chain of indebtedness. As this chain expands, you get a powerful social group.

From this we see that friendship depends on actions in the same way that dance depends upon movement. When the action or movement stops, so does the dance. When the friendship actions stop, so does the friendship. It may linger for a while but end it does.

What is the most effective way to forge friendships? It takes more than sending Facebook messages. Instead, incorporate the lessons of all three Hebrew words. Be creative and diligent in discovering ways to do favors for others, but at the same time be willing to ask for and accept favors too. Allow a two way flow of kindness-actions between you and those you wish to befriend. In good times, and even more in difficult ones, nobody can have too many friends.

THOUGHT TOOL

5

PASSOVER AND THE PACIFIC CROSSING

**Stress makes it easy to ignore the
other important parts of life.**

To the dismay of my parents and the bewilderment of my wife Susan's parents, we sailed our family from Los Angeles to Honolulu on our small sailboat a few years ago. We spent nearly a year in preparation. Susan planned the meals for the entire voyage and wrote down where each item of food was stored, while I strengthened the vessel and polished my celestial navigation skills. We departed on the fourth of July and by mid-month we were about a thousand miles from the West Coast and the same distance from Hawaii.

That night, as usual, I measured our water supply and in an exhausted state from too many hours on watch mistakenly determined that we had only one more day's water left. In a terrible panic, all I could think about was how would I keep my family alive till we reached Hawaii. In my mind that became the only problem.

However, in reality all the other challenges of crossing the Pacific in a small boat hadn't vanished; they'd merely been eclipsed. I still had to locate the tiny speck of Oahu in a vast ocean; we still had to feed our crew, and we still had to avoid collisions. But in the middle of that dark and frightening night I could only think about what we would drink.

Stress makes it easy to ignore all the other important parts of life. In the dark gloom of financial need, family relationships are easily sacrificed. We neglect physical exercise in the gnawing worry of want. Whether its source is health, finances, family or something else, stress has a way of looming large enough to overwhelm all other parts of life. The annual Passover holyday offers a clue to coping.

The Egyptians enslaved and oppressed the Jews. You would have thought that God would get them out of Egypt as quickly as possible. Yet first, each Israelite family was to take a lamb, roast it and prepare for the first Seder. You'd have expected a chorus of protest from the Israelites: "C'mon God, get us out of here – there'll be plenty of time for lamb barbecues once we're in the desert."

Instead, they first had to sit down for the formal Passover meal, each family with its father at the table. Why couldn't this family celebration have been postponed? Furthermore God instructed the Israelites to go and gather all the money owed them by the Egyptians. That had to take quite some time. Yet no Israelite is recorded to have said, "Forget about the money, God, just get us out of this Egyptian hell-hole."

In order for the big problem of slavery and oppression to be solved, we first had to address smaller problems like religious ritual, family affirmation, and yes, money. During centuries in Egypt, just surviving put people under so much pressure that families fell apart, finances fell apart and they seldom connected with God through religious practice.

God's Passover statement was, "Look, I'll get you out of here but you need to do your part too – first recapture all the important aspects of your life which you've neglected. Fathers get back to building your families, reconnect with God and focus on the finances."

If you have a big problem, keep on the program with the other stuff. Take care of your body and take care of your relationships with family and friends. Keep your spiritual life healthy as you chip away at your financial challenges. Don't let stress in one area eclipse the rest of your life. Solving money problems won't be easier if you lose your health. Resolving family dilemmas won't be easier if your finances go south. And nothing will be easier if you write-off your relationship with God.

Oh, and that water problem on the boat? Well, I remembered the ancient Jewish wisdom I have imparted here and realized that sacrificing sleep was going to leave me less capable of dealing with the problem; not more. I prayed, and in the process of moving my mind away from the problem onto my relationship with God I recalled that every can of fruit and vegetables on board contained some liquid. That already sent me to bed with an easier mind.

When I awoke I discovered that I had measured the water level incorrectly and we had plenty of water after all. When tackled as part of the bigger picture, some problems even vanish.

6

HOW TO BE HER MAIN MAN

How do a husband and wife create a unified single entity?

Couples must struggle to establish themselves as one, indivisible unit. It is tough for a man to learn that his wife is entitled to know of his whereabouts at all times. It is tough for a woman to learn that how she dresses is now also her husband's business. How do a husband and wife create a unified single entity?

Wisdom and advice for living leap from the pages of the Bible. Scripture is never only about the narrative. Vital secrets to life are embedded in stories such as this one:

Once upon a time, there lived a princess named Michal. She was the daughter of King Saul and married a young hero named David. Later David became king of Israel and arranged for the Ark of the Covenant to return home.

And as the ark of the Lord entered the City
of David, Michal, <u>the daughter of Saul</u>, looked
through a window and saw King David dancing
and leaping before God and she had
contempt for him in her heart.

(Samuel II 6:16)

How could the wife of King David despise her husband? Ancient Jewish wisdom shows how the answer emerges from the text. She is identified as, "Michal, the daughter of Saul," rather than as, "Michal, the wife of David."

Something has gone very wrong. David has failed to become the main man in Michal's life. She was more "daughter of Saul" than she was "wife of David."

That chapter ends with these poignant words:

> And Michal _the daughter of Saul_ had
> no children till the day she died.

Since Michal's main man was clearly not David, the marriage was lacking and unable to bear fruit. Where did David and Michal go wrong? Was she ever "Michal, wife of David"?

At the time of their marriage described in Samuel I 18:28, Michal is described as "Michal the daughter of Saul" but this is not disturbing. She is a newly married wife and still sees herself as daughter of her father.

Later she saves her husband's life, and for the first time we see that David has truly won his princess:

> And _Michal, David's wife_ told him,
> 'If you do not flee tonight, tomorrow you die.'
> (I Samuel 19:11)

Michal defies her father and saves her husband's life; we are not surprised to see that their marriage has now developed to the happy point where she sees herself as David's wife.

As the battle between King Saul and his son-in-law escalates, in Samuel I chapter 25, Saul takes "Michal his daughter" and gives her to another man. Well, if her father is seizing her from her husband and forcing her on another man, naturally she would be called "Michal the daughter of Saul."

The tide of battle turns and Avner, who had been a staunch military supporter of Saul, approaches David wanting to ally with him. David tells Avner that there will be no discussion until Michal is returned to him. Here comes David's mistake:

> ...you will not see my face until you first bring me
> Michal, _daughter of Saul_.
>
> (Samuel II 3:13)

David should have insisted "Bring me Michal, my wife."

Ancient Jewish wisdom lets us know that David viewed her as a political asset not as his wife. He fails to restore Michal to the role she played as his wife on that day she saved his life.

We can now understand how she was able to feel contempt for her husband. Tragically, she had again become Michal, daughter of Saul.

A man yearns for his wife's respect, and a wife needs a husband she can respect. However, if he demands respect, he merely transforms himself into a buffoon. Husbands must learn how to acquire that respect and the lesson of David is that the responsibility for creating and keeping that respect is primarily the husband's.

The unity of the marriage depends upon the husband earning

and retaining his wife's respect and becoming her main man. How does he do it? Three steps that are quicker to state than to integrate into one's being. First, he demonstrates constant and consistent respect for his wife. Second, he demonstrates constant and consistent self-discipline. Finally, he demonstrates constant and consistent care for the welfare of his wife and children. This way, he'll be her main man forever.

7

HAVE I GOT A DEAL FOR YOU!

How do you tell good salesmanship from deceit?

M ost adults have faced the crushing experience of being cheated by someone we trusted. It might have been a close friend or we may have fallen for the claims of an unethical salesman.

We walk a tightrope between wanting to remain trusting and optimistic in our dealings with others, while at the same time not wishing to be exploited.

God put us all into a "Garden of Eden" to work it and look after it (Genesis 2:15). One of our missions is to extract a living from an often reluctant earth. God thus ordained it because by making our own living in an honest and ethical manner, we can't help but benefit other human beings. But there truly is no free lunch.

If we train ourselves to resist trying to get something for nothing and we realize that anything that seems too good to be true usually is, we can better protect ourselves. Becoming alert to deceitful language is an important skill that Scripture teaches us. Let's watch a con man in action:

In a complicated few verses, Shechem, the son of Hamor, rapes Jacob's daughter, Dina, and then wishes to marry her. Hamor speaks to Jacob and his sons.

> *Intermarry with us; your daughters you will give to us and our daughters you will take for yourselves.*
> (Genesis 34:9)

If, for the moment, we ignore the fact that Dina was already forcibly taken, this seems to be quite a generous offer. Hamor offers Jacob and his sons a deal that will allow them to retain control of the relationship. Jacob and his sons will give their daughters and take the daughters of Hamor's city, but only if they choose to do so.

Things seem quite different only a few verses later, when Hamor and his son Shechem speak to their own people. This time they say:

> *...their daughters we will take for ourselves as wives and our daughters we will give to them.*
> (Genesis 34: 20-21)

Who is in control now?

There is another difference between how Hamor speaks to Jacob's family and to his own people. He mentions to both parties that in addition to intermarriage, there will be economic benefits in joining up. However, he reverses the order.

To Jacob's family, upset at the way Dina was treated, the emphasis is on marriage. Economics are secondary. In talking to his own people, the financial ramifications are given priority followed by the marriage incentive.

Ancient Jewish wisdom labels the first change in language as deceitful, but not the second. What can we learn?

By promising each faction that it alone would be in control of the marriages, Hamor reveals himself as a liar. He cannot fulfill one promise without breaking the other. They contradict each other. Salesmen or politicians who commit to certain things while speaking to one group and commit to exactly the opposite while speaking to another are deceitful and dangerous.

But in stressing marriage over economics or vice versa, Hamor isn't doing anything wrong. If you are selling your house and focus on proximity to schools for a couple with children and on local golf courses to an older couple, you are simply paying attention to each one's interests. As long as there are both schools and golf courses, you are behaving ethically.

Making a profit, getting elected or getting married can all be achieved honestly or through underhanded tactics. It is important to learn how to interpret language and recognize signs of deceit in all our human interactions. Monitoring our own language and behavior allows us to flourish economically while relating with faithfulness and integrity toward others.

8

BLOOD, SWEAT AND MONEY?

How we think about money
very much impacts our ability to create it.

Have you noticed that people say things like, "Open communication is the lifeblood of this organization," or "A reliable fuel supply is the lifeblood of this airline?" But they seldom say, "New members are the gall bladder of this club" or, "Busy bureaucrats are the big toe of government." What is so special about blood?

Like Superman swooping in to the rescue, here comes ancient Jewish wisdom with the answer.

Regular readers of Thought Tools know that in the Lord's language, Hebrew, when one word is used for two apparently separate concepts, those two ideas are really very connected to one another.

The Hebrew word for blood DAMIM is identical to one of the words used throughout the ancient writings of Jewish wisdom to mean money.

Blood = DAMIM = Money

What are the similarities between blood and money?

Both money and blood are most useful in quantity. The singular of both words is seldom used. "I need some blood," but never, "I need a blood." "Can you lend me a money?" No, I don't think so.

Blood and money both comprise countless individual elements, each one identifiable, but needing to be aggregated with many others to be useful. Blood is made up of countless units called red and white cells and money is made up of countless units like pennies or dollars.

Both blood and money are relatively fungible. When you borrow my car, I want that car returned, not a similar one. When you pay me back the ten dollars I loaned you on Friday, I really don't care that it is not exactly the same $10 bill I gave you. In fact, you can even write me a check.

Organs like a heart or liver often get rejected when transferred from one person to another, which makes transplants very challenging. Blood, however, can be moved from person to person with comparative ease just like money.

Both blood and money need to circulate in order to be effective. Bags of blood can contribute to human health; but merely sitting on the shelf in the blood bank they aren't doing their job. It is just the same for bags of money. They are not doing anyone any good merely sitting on the shelf in the money bank. That is why when people fearfully hoard their dollars rather than spending or investing them, our economy totters.

Finally, both blood and money carry nourishment to the furthest reaches of the organism whether a country or a body. If blood is cut off from an extremity of the body, like a toe, the toe will die. When a customer in Maine buys goods from a seller in the remote foothills of the Rockies, the entire country thrives.

The medium of exchange necessary for that transaction is money. When a craftsman in Africa sells a bracelet to a teacher in England, money has made that craftsman healthier just like a blood transfusion would.

By using the identical word for blood and money, ancient Jewish wisdom teaches that our money is indeed our life-blood and must be treated every bit as seriously as our real blood. For instance, a hemorrhage of either entity must be stopped and treated immediately. Tainted blood and tainted money both have the power to destroy life. Unfortunately, many of us fail to take financial first aid as seriously as we do medical first aid.

Wrapping your inner soul around the idea that your money IS your lifeblood is step one in becoming fiscally healthier. How we think about money very much impacts our ability to create it.

MEN, MONEY AND MARRIAGE

**Say you're on a date and the guy asks you
to split the bill. What do you do?**

Hello! It's the twenty-first century already. Yet I recently read an 'advice to the lovelorn' column that could have come out of 1950, or for that matter, 1850. The girl wrote in asking how she should react to a man who asked her to split the restaurant check after a date. The columnist responded that the girl should have nothing further to do with that scoundrel.

I was nonplussed. Today many women work in high paying jobs, yet the columnist didn't even address this issue. It didn't seem fair to me. The guy failed to foot the bill so he was kicked to the curb.

Surprised by the answer, I asked several single women: "Say you're on a date and the guy asks you to split the bill. What do you do?"

To my astonishment, each answered the same way. She'd never see him again. How interesting! As modern times dawned, women started wearing pants. Women started smoking cigarettes. Women entered every imaginable profession. Goodness gracious, women even went into space.

But somehow, asking a woman to pay for her own meal is an unforgivable breach of etiquette. What is going on here?

As usual, for solutions to life's mysteries, I turn to the Book that has had more to do with shaping western civilization than any other volume. In passing, let me tell you that we are living in the first generation to consider itself educated while being utterly ignorant of the Bible. Knowing nothing of the Bible, these folks dismiss the Book which has offered wisdom to smart men and women for millennia as nothing but primitive superstition.

To be sure, some old ideas are superstitious. But others are supremely wise. Let me tell you the difference between superstition and wisdom. When a man becomes terrified of going to work because he spotted a black cat on the way to the bus stop, he is a superstitious fool.

When someone sees a ladder leaning against the wall on the sidewalk ahead of him, and he deliberately walks around the base of the ladder rather than under it, he is practicing wisdom.

Over the course of many years, people discovered that walking beneath a ladder increases the likelihood of being struck on the head by a hammer or can of paint dropped by a careless workman aloft. Information in the Bible is closer to the ladder analogy than the black cat story.

Over the course of many years, smart people have found the Bible to contain permanent principles of how the world really works. Were this not the case, the Bible would hardly be the most popular book in the world.

What does this have to do with men paying for dates in today's day and age?

For those of us who believe that the Bible contains permanent principles of how the world really works, details in the Bible matter, including why Adam preceded Eve in the Garden of Eden. God could just as easily have created Eve first, or both together.

Ancient Jewish wisdom explains that the Eden account of Adam preceding Eve is to teach us a vital lesson.

By the nature of things, when a woman marries a man, she agrees to make herself vulnerable and enters her husband's garden, as it were. If she does her husband the honor of allowing him to support her, she becomes vulnerable. If she agrees to devote many of her energies to building a home instead of building her own career, she becomes vulnerable. If she becomes pregnant, she becomes vulnerable.

It is thus perfectly natural for a smart single woman to measure her date's financial ability and graciousness. Will he feel that taking care of her is a privilege and a thrill? Will he treat her with less respect and consideration if her contributions to the relationship and the family don't involve a paycheck? She needs answers to this and other questions before making any commitment. Permanent principles never change and fortunately for us the ancient Jewish wisdom on men, money and marriage is revealed in the first few chapters of Genesis.

10

DO YOU REMEMBER?

**Why would God link the concept of
memory to males?**

Memory is among those easily overlooked gifts for
which we ought to offer up daily gratitude to God.

Without memory, one is isolated from others. But even
worse, one is isolated from oneself. Without memory, life is
a disconnected sequence of thinly sliced moments of time.
It is memory that stitches together those instants, compiling
them into our identity.

The word "re-member" means to join together just as the
word "dis-member" means to separate.

Loss of family memory is also a tragedy. Happy memories
help unify families. Creating a repository of good times
spurs smiles and a strong sense of connection when those
memories are later shared.

Institutional memory is a real asset for a business. My friend,
Dave Ramsey, America's herald of hope, emphasizes how
companies must teach their new employees the story of
how the business began. To this day, employees of Bank of
America are inspired by the memory of Amadeo Giannini

keeping his two year-old bank open during the aftermath of San Francisco's 1906 earthquake, while other bankers fled the ruined city.

Similarly, a country's citizens are sustained by a collective memory of how and why their nation's founders struggled. Only by knowing their shared history can people share a destiny.

Not surprisingly, Scripture repeatedly directs Israel to remember. Numerous verses in the Five Books of Moses stress the act of remembering. Take a look at this general admonition:

Remember the days gone by
(Deuteronomy 32:7)

Ancient Jewish wisdom offers a crucial clue to the nature of memory. In the Lord's language, if two concepts share the same word, those two concepts are connected. It is significant that Hebrew uses only one word for both male and memory. In both the sentences below, I have copied how the underlined word looks in the original Hebrew. It doesn't matter if you don't read Hebrew; simply compare the shapes of the letters.

So God created Man in His image...
<u>*male*</u> *(ZaCHaR) and female he created them.*
(Genesis 1:27)

Male

And the butler did not remember
(ZaCHaR) Joseph, he forgot him.

(Genesis 40:23)

זכר
Remember

Now why, by using the same word for male and remember, would God link the concept of memory to males? We can better understand this by asking what the difference is between males and females when it comes to memory.

Well, one of the most significant differences between the sexes is that most girls naturally grow into womanhood, while many boys, if neglected, will either remain adolescents or become barbarians. Surely you know more forty year-old males who are still adolescents, than females? Transforming boys into men takes effort.

While most girls intuitively feel the desire to devote themselves to one man and instinctively know how to cuddle a baby, for a society to endure, boys must be taught how men should behave.

Girls mature with an inbuilt awareness of time while boys tend to live only for the moment. This makes them act destructively toward themselves and also toward their community. The cure for this is memory which links a boy to his father and to the uplifting traditions of manhood.

Boys desperately need role models of manly behavior from the past. Heroic accounts of brave and chivalrous men inspire boys, encouraging them to adopt similar behaviors. Memory is vital for males to become men, which is why families use the father's name rather than the mother's.

While unfortunately, not every boy receives the needed education from his family or community, one resource, the Bible, is available to all. In the earliest chapters of Genesis, God establishes the ground rules for male behavior. As I discuss in my audio CD, Madam I'm Adam: Decoding the Marriage Secrets of Eden, even the first usage of the Hebrew word for man appears in a surprising location, delivering a potent message.

Loss of memory is a dreadful affliction. Medical science has not yet found the solution. However, we can do much to create and maintain memories in our families and in our businesses. We can also play our small roles in helping the young males in our communities aspire to successful lives.

11

WORK BETTER BY NOT WORKING

**God created a world with rhythms and cycles.
When we defy them we function less effectively.**

I sleep pretty regularly. I climb into bed and nod off for somewhere between five and eight hours, seven nights a week. That is a lot of unproductive time yet nobody has ever asked me, "Why do you repeatedly waste almost a full work week's worth of hours doing nothing but sleeping?" Everyone understands that though sleep might look like a waste of time, it benefits my body. It makes me more effective, not less.

However, folks do constantly ask how I justify wasting twenty-five hours every week by observing the Sabbath. From sunset on Friday evening until nightfall on Saturday, my family and I do not use our cars, computers, phones or faxes. We don't even use our pencils and pens. We eschew electronic entertainment in all forms neither listening to radio nor watching television. We don't do laundry or other chores.

Instead, we enjoy three sumptuous Sabbath meals. On Friday night, at Saturday lunch time, and again later during Saturday afternoon, we sit down to a leisurely repast with family and friends, enjoying food, fellowship and uplifting conversation. We spend a little more time on prayer than we do on other days, and our sleep is a little more restful. Though to some my Sabbath might look like a waste of time, it benefits my soul. It makes me more effective, not less.

God created a world with rhythms and cycles and when we defy them we function less effectively. For instance, jet lag overwhelms us when we try to override the circadian rhythm built into our bodies by quickly crossing time zones.

One of the most compelling natural rhythms that God built into nature is that powerful processes seldom occur in lengthy, uninterrupted, unidirectional thrusts. Think of breathing. We do not breathe by means of a never ceasing suction system. Our noses could have operated like little vacuum cleaners, just gently sucking in air, non-stop, day and night. We could periodically expel the carbon dioxide our body produces just as we periodically expel other waste our bodies produce. Instead, we breathe in and then out. In and out, exert and relax, air out and air in, push and retreat, all our lives.

Why do we sleep? Though many theories exist, nobody really knows. All I can tell you is that it fits God's pattern for productive processes; exert and relax, advance and retreat, wake and sleep.

Most productive human interactions work similarly, for example, conversation. How exhausting and unproductive it is to be spoken at endlessly. Conversation works best when we talk and then listen. Again the same pattern of exert and withdraw. The same is true for the productive processes of both conception and birth. During the latter, contractions squeeze the expectant mother then there is a pause before the next exertion.

In the late 19th century, Thomas Edison built an electrical power station in Manhattan and lit up local streets and buildings. The kind of electricity he used was Direct Current or DC. This means that electrons constantly keep pushing and exerting in the same direction. But soon the world switched to Nikola Tesla's Alternating Current, or AC, in which the electrons push and then retreat, push again and then back off. Alternating current works better. Why wouldn't it? After all, it fits the natural rhythms of God's world.

Here is a graph of alternating current.

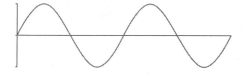

Do you see how similar it looks to that green wave on the electronic monitor next to a hospital patient's bed? First up in one direction and then down in the reverse direction, push and retreat, exert and relax. That is how the world works.

Remember the Sabbath day in order to make it holy.
For six days you must exert and achieve all
your creativity. And the seventh day is Sabbath
for the Lord your God, do not achieve
any creativity....

(Exodus 20:8-10)

Do you see the two component parts of the Sabbath? For six days we push and exert – that is part one. Part two decrees one day of retreat and withdraw. That is how the world works and that is one of the most vital rhythms built into our souls.

By celebrating a Sabbath we can look inwards rather than outwards, and we can enjoy and absorb rather than exert and generate. It is a withdrawal from the hectic pace of active life and a period of introspection after which we are able to return to creative work and intense exertion with renewed energy and refreshed ambition.

12

BASEBALL, IDOLS AND TYRANNY

Life is more fun when you know
the rules of the game.

When I first arrived in the United States everything I saw thrilled me – except baseball. Having been raised on a game called cricket, which is only slightly more exciting than watching grass grow, I found the rules of baseball hard to grasp.

Soon after radio host Michael Medved and I started our exciting young congregation in Venice, California, I was invited to play on the synagogue softball team. I quickly learned my lesson. Games are more fun when you know the rules. The same is true for life.

The difference between baseball and life is that when you insist on playing ball while ignoring the rules, you are soon ejected from the team. However, when you do the same in life, you are often hailed as a brave pioneer shattering tired old conventions with your fearless forays into foolishness.

I recall parents who earnestly invited their offspring to call them by their first names. "We want our kids to see us as their best friends," they told me. I suggested that children want parents, not big tall friends and that the

Fifth Commandment was one of the rules of the game.

Another rule of the game of life is not to worship idols or false gods. Now what possible relevance could that have for us today? After all, when last did you see someone sneak off for some illicit praying time at the local temple of Ba'al? When last did you open a closet at your friend's home and discover his stash of idols?

Well, of course, carved idols are only one example of idolatry. We think of them as primitive. But just because we are more sophisticated does not mean that we have escaped the sinister seduction of idolatry. We all tend to worship false gods; they're just not made of wood and stone.

Worshiping a false god means choosing as the guiding compass of your life something other than God's message to humanity. There is Edith whose entire life is dedicated to creating bamboo art work. Marriage, family and health are all subservient concerns. Art is not a part of her life – it is her life. Art is her false god. Not surprisingly, she is divorced and estranged from her children.

Foster venerates academia. The way he judges people by this sole criterion has distanced him from his talented, artistic daughter. His obsession has even ruined his career as he ignores good ideas that are offered by colleagues who lack Ivy League degrees. He has chosen his idol and he worships it.

When you don't know the rules of baseball yet you persist in playing, your ignorance soon becomes apparent. Perceptive eyes can also see when you don't know the rules of life. Anyone watching Edith and Foster knows that their false gods are ruining their lives.

The Bible uses different Hebrew words for idols. One is PeSeL which means 'engraved' or 'carved.' This word hints at the compelling power of false gods. Once one embraces an idol in one's life, it is a powerful force engraved upon one's soul.

Another word for idol is ETZeV.

> *And they (the Philistines) left their <u>idols</u> there,*
> *and David and his men burned them.*
> (II Samuel 5:21)

עֲצַב
idol

However, this is exactly the same word as used in this verse:

> *Like a deserted wife, <u>sorrowful</u> in spirit*
> (Isaiah 54:6)

עֲצַב
sorrow

So one word in Hebrew means both idol and sorrow? Exactly! We all live our lives according to certain rules. If we ignore or distort God's rules, following false paths, or an ETZeV, the result is increased sorrow, ETZeV in our lives.

Yes, life is more fun for you and everyone around you when you know the rules of the game.

13

THE PILGRIMS AND ROSH HASHANA

**Once the Pilgrims switched to private
ownership and enterprise was rewarded,
the colony began to flourish.**

While Rosh HaShana, the start of the Jewish year, is usually observed about two months before Thanksgiving, the holyday raises thoughts of the Pilgrims.

Those who sailed on the Mayflower were deeply religious and Biblically knowledgeable Christians. So it is astounding that in setting up the Plymouth Plantation, they agreed to an arrangement with their merchant sponsors that contradicted a vital Bible principle.

According to the terms of their agreement, the land and whatever the settlers built or produced belonged to the group in common, not to individuals. That idea was a miserable failure. Hard working members resented working to benefit the lazy. Why put in greater effort for no greater gain? Once they switched to private ownership and enterprise was rewarded, the colony began to flourish.

In the words of William Bradford, second governor of the colony, they initially acted as if, "they were wiser than God." Bad move.

Throughout the Torah, God's word consistently emphasizes that private property is to be respected. Whether it is Abraham's insistence on buying the land for Sarah's burial, or the overwhelming number of Biblical verses that deal with economic transactions, God's message to humanity elevates ownership. Charity itself is only possible if people own something; you can only give from what belongs to you.

Not only do we need to respect private property, ancient Jewish wisdom even disdains ownerless objects; for instance lost objects.

Look at the following words:

> *...and so you shall do for all objects which have been lost...you cannot hide.*
> (Deut. 22:3)

There you are power walking down the street on your way to an appointment, when out of the corner of your eye you spot a bracelet lying on the ground. Remarkably, God does not allow you the option of ignoring the lost bracelet and simply passing it by. Just by seeing that item which has both value and unique properties, you have become its caretaker. You are now obligated to search for its owner. Returning lost objects to their owners is a commandment, not a suggestion.

What does this have to do with Rosh HaShana, a time of judgment, repentance and fresh starts?

At this time of year we emphasize that we have been lost; separated from our Owner. However, unlike objects, which don't have the power to actualize their own return, human beings can indeed do so.

The Rosh HaShana worship service speaks of yearning for a time when all creation recognizes that God is our Creator. Once we acknowledge that He alone owns the world, recognizing His role in judging us and repenting for disobeying His rules follows naturally.

As our Creator, God allows us the use of our bodies and of His wonderful world. The obligation is on us to leave both better off than when we received them. After all, you may certainly borrow a car, but you can't drive it recklessly. Even better is to wash it and fill up the gas tank before returning it.

Furthermore, we weren't lost because of our Owner's inattention. We ourselves wandered away and are responsible for heading back home. Fortunately, we have been given a guidebook, the Bible, to highlight the path. Since we each have value and unique properties, we cannot hide.

The five books of Moses are divided into 54 sections. Jews read one section (sometimes 2) each week. The Shabbat before Rosh HaShana, we read the section known as Nitzavim, which includes chapter 30 of Deuteronomy. In the first ten verses, the root word "SHaV," or "return" appears seven times.

Like the Pilgrims we will only benefit from not trying to be wiser than God.

14

FINGER POINTING 101

Do not use one weight to judge ourselves leniently, while using a harsher weight when judging someone else.

Have you ever been put down by a silent sneer? Have you ever sensed harsh criticism in nothing more than a raised eyebrow? Have you ever felt your value as a person, as a friend, or as a relative minimized by someone finding fault in you or dismissing an achievement of yours as insignificant?

We've all been hurt by insults and criticism. Now, how about the other way around? Do you find too much fault with others? Do your children fear telling you of their activities and their thoughts? Are you far more lavish with criticism than praise?

If so, though you may be unaware, your friends, family and co-workers may subconsciously avoid having to spend more time with you than they absolutely must.

If so, you are dogged by invisible forces that impede your progress. They place barriers in your way and suck the joy out of your existence. When life is good, it is often because you are surrounded by individuals who like you and want things to go well for you. They place opportunities in your way, they introduce you to people you should meet, and they correct false impressions about you. All of this takes place beyond your awareness.

However when the individuals who populate the broader reaches of your life view you as constantly critical, they may respect you, they may love you but they feel less comfortable with you. Naturally, they do not go out of their way to help you.

Though they may not do anything actually to hurt you, merely the absence of their active support translates into hidden specters that obstruct much of what you seek in life. The good news is that you can change this.

Ancient Jewish wisdom offers this helpful gem. In every interaction, give the other person the benefit of the doubt, the support and the praise that you would want him to give you if the situation was reversed. Be as generous in judging the actions of others as you tend to be when judging your own actions.

Let me explain with the help of Scripture:

> *You shall do no evil in judgment in matters*
> *of length, weight, or volume. You shall have*
> *just scales, just weights, a just measure for dry*
> *goods, and a just measure for liquids...*
> (Leviticus 19:35-36)

In other words, we may not use a fraudulently light weight when we sell and a heavier one when we buy. God wants us to do business with scrupulous honesty. That seems perfectly clear, doesn't it? This seems to make the following verses redundant:

> *You may not have in your pocket two weights,*
> *a heavy one and a light one. You may not have*
> *in your house two measures, a larger one and a*
> *smaller one. Only one full and just weight shall*
> *you have and only one full and just measure...*
> (Deuteronomy 25:13-16)

Ancient Jewish wisdom explains that the Deuteronomy verses go beyond commerce. These verses are talking of false weights, not in the market place, but in our pockets and homes. These verses teach us not to use one weight or measure by judging ourselves leniently and a different harsher weight or measure when judging someone else.

The process of changing and improving me involves banishing my old self and is called Atonement. It requires that I bring my actions into alignment with my self-image; in other words, becoming one integrated personality

When you find yourself about to put someone down with a silent sneer or a raised eyebrow, or whenever you are about to find fault with someone, remember to use only one set of weights and measures. You will astound your friends, please your family and delight those who share your workplace.

15

TREACHEROUS WATERS

**Not knowing where you are means that you have
no idea of the direction in which to steer.**

There we were; my wife, Susan and our seven children
aboard a smallish boat about to cross the Strait of Georgia
in British Columbia. We were departing Vancouver's False
Creek bound for Porlier Pass about 30 miles away.

Would it be all right if I give you a very basic course on
navigation? You take your chart (which landlubbers call
a map) and identify your current position – False Creek.
Then you draw a line from there to your destination – Porlier
Pass, just north of beautiful Galiano Island.

Using the nautical chart's compass rose, you discover that
you must steer a course of 220 degrees. In theory, things
are simple. You start the engines, untie the boat from the
dock, leave the harbor and maintain your course.

Actually, not so simple. You need to take into account
a strong northerly tidal flow that pushes up the Strait of
Georgia. Otherwise, by the time you are half-way across
you will have no idea where you are. Not knowing where
you are means that you have no idea of the direction in
which to steer to reach your destination – or how to avoid

shallow water or other hazards.

A core concept of motivational and management training is identifying goals. However there is a more basic need. You first must accurately identify your current location. If you don't know where you are, you have absolutely no idea how to get where you want to be.

Ancient Jewish wisdom reveals this timeless truth.

When Adam hid from God among the trees of the garden, God called him and said, "AYeKa," or in English:

Where are you?

(Genesis 3:9)

אַיֶּכָּה

Everyone reading those lines from Genesis asks the obvious question: What kind of question is that? Certainly, God knew where Adam was.

We see the answer by looking at the first word in the book off Lamentations, – AYKha – which translates as "how."

אֵיכָה

How lonely sits the city that was so full of
people – she has become like a widow.

(Lamentations 1:1)

That looks pretty similar to the word God used to question Adam, doesn't it?

If you have learned from any of my Genesis Journey CDs you probably know that the Tanach, the Hebrew Bible is written without vowels – those strange looking little dots and lines around the letters. The exact same combination of letters can sound differently and have different meaning depending on its pronunciation in each instance.

To fully understand any Hebrew word, all possible words its letters could make need to be considered. For instance, if English was God's language, *pan*, *pen*, *pin*, *pun*, not to mention *pine* and *open* would all be written "pn." To understand what any one of them means, you would need to understand all of them. What is ridiculous in English is eye-opening in Hebrew. All the implications of a word must be considered rather than only the particular meaning implied by one particular arrangement of vowels.

You can see that ignoring vowels as we ought to, "Where are you?" from Genesis is exactly the same arrangement of letters as the word that opens Lamentations. These four letters give the book its name in Hebrew and wherever that word appears it heralds impending trouble.

What is the connection? The magic of Hebrew is telling us that not knowing where we are leads to rocky waters ahead, to the lament of despair. God was not asking Adam to reveal his hiding place. He was telling Adam that he was spiritually lost; "Where are you, Adam?"

Setting goals is wonderful. You cannot lead a family, business or nation without doing so. But in order to reach the goal, you need a brutally honest assessment of where you are right now.

WEIGHTLESS WORK

**The Kehatis lifted the Ark with joy in their hearts
and a song on their lips.**

Terry really didn't feel like mowing the lawn. Nevertheless, he cranked up the mower and got to work. For the first half hour Terry grumbled. During the next half hour, he was silent. An hour into the job, he began to whistle and then to sing. When the job was done and his lawn looked like a golf green, Terry was so elated he was sorry his work was finished.

Just occasionally, when we undertake a much detested duty, we find the task sweeping us along in a rapture of enthusiasm. Wouldn't it be useful if we knew how to approach all our tasks so they lift us and carry us along to completion as a cresting wave carries the ebullient surfer towards the shore?

The problem is that our heads tell us to perform necessary assignments, while our hearts sink at the prospect. One way to help our heads defeat our hearts is to make the task inject energy *into us*, rather than drain it *from us*.

The Bible yields a clue. Stephen Langton, a thirteenth century Archbishop of Canterbury, divided the Five Books of Moses into the system of chapters most of us follow today. Using only his own logic, he set where chapters would begin and end.

However, there is a God-given system which divides the Torah into fifty-four *sidrahs*, each containing several chapters. We gain glimpses into God's mind by identifying the comprehensive theme of each sidrah. This motif which is always linked to the official name of the sidrah, can be easily missed when one of Langton's chapters unwittingly includes the end of one sidrah and the beginning of the next.

Chapter four of the book of Numbers describes a simple set of instructions for counting the families of the three sons of Levi: Kehat, Gershon and Merari. But, when we look at the book of Numbers according to the sidrah system, a different story emerges.

The second sidrah of the Book of Numbers actually opens with verse 21, right in the middle of chapter four. The sidrah's opening topic is the counting of the families of two of the three sons of Levi, namely Gershon and Merari. Their brother Kehat's counting takes place earlier, at the end of the first sidrah. Why are the three families separated by a sidrah break?

We get a clue from the fact that each sidrah is named, not numbered. The sidrah that includes the two families is named Naso, which means carrying. This sidrah includes an account of six wagons being allocated to the Gershonites and Merarites for transporting the vessels and components of the Tabernacle. Intriguingly, no wagons are assigned to the family of Kehat who was to carry the Ark of the Covenant upon their shoulders.

Ancient Jewish wisdom teaches that there are different types of carrying. Gershon and Merari needed wagons not only because of what they carried but because of a subtle flaw in their attitude. Sometimes their assignment felt like a burden. In contrast, the Kehatis lifted the Ark with joy in their hearts and a song on their lips. Not only was the Ark no burden to them, but it actually provided them with extra energy, in effect carrying them. No wonder they couldn't be included in the same sidrah as their brothers' families, in the sidrah called "Carrying." They weren't carrying – they were being carried and therefore needed no wagons.

Similarly, in each of our lives there are daily responsibilities to discharge. Diapers need to be changed, products and services need to be sold, and arduous travel needs to be undertaken. What is in our control is our attitude. We can approach these tasks as burdens beneath which we groan and which drain away our energies. Alternatively, we can tackle them the way the ambitious athlete approaches a marathon or a gym workout. Launching ourselves at our tasks like happy warriors helps to turn these tasks into weightless opportunities which can carry us, giving us energy and joy.

DEATH BY LONELINESS

**Despite a unique relationship with God,
Adam still was bereft without another person.**

*Twelve women shot in a fitness center by a man the
New York Times called '...tortured by loneliness.'*

*Thirty-two victims shot at Virginia Tech by a man the New
York Times described as '...consumed by a troubling silence.'*

*Thirteen people killed in a Binghamton social center
by a gunman the same newspaper labeled
'...an introvert who was secretive in the extreme.'*

Murder is an extreme and thankfully rare response to
excruciating loneliness. Nonetheless, while most of
us do not react violently to the pain of disconnectedness,
we still suffer.

We might have hundreds of friends, belong to clubs, churches
or synagogues, and be at a different social engagement every
night. We might even be married and still overwhelmed by
the anguish of loneliness. It is not the quantity of people you
know; it is the quality of the connections with them.

Being without authentic human contact does to our souls exactly what starvation does to our bodies. God created us with obvious physical needs but He also created us with spiritual needs. Connectedness with others is a spiritual necessity and being deprived of it harms us just as surely as deprivation of food.

You may well have experienced this very problem without diagnosing it. Perhaps you feel a subtle difficulty at summoning up feelings of happiness. Perhaps you feel a little depressed and can think of nothing that would make you happy. The first and most likely explanation is insufficient authentic connection with other people.

Ancient Jewish wisdom helps explain what authentic connection is. It was first achieved in that most perfect of all places, the Garden of Eden. After saying, "It is not good for man to be alone," God solved the problem by creating Eve. This powerful message reminds us that despite a unique relationship with God, Adam still was bereft without another person. In Eden, Adam and Eve shared an environment of spiritual compatibility. Their shared world-view made possible authentic connection.

But sin brought life in the Garden to an end. Their eviction from paradise left their descendants, including us, needing to build an artificial garden of shared values. Real connection is found with people with whom we share beliefs rather than interests.

After driving Adam and Eve out, God placed two Cherubs east of Eden, guarding the way to the Tree of Life. Their purpose was to protect the pathway into paradise, leaving us with an urgent question. How can those two cherubs guide us back to Eden and help banish loneliness?

If you are becoming familiar with the Torah technology I teach, you know that it is significant that we encounter the two cherubs in only one other circumstance throughout the entire Five Books of Moses. They are found upon the gold lid of the Ark of the Covenant, in Exodus 25:18 and 37:7.

Their reappearance there is the ultimate clue. The avenue back to Eden is through the Biblical blueprint contained within the box guarded by the cherubs. The same cherubs that protect the path to Eden also point the way to God's laws contained within the ark, which provide a common framework for relationships.

This is why the cherubs never appear as individuals but only as a pair. They are the very metaphor of friendship and connection. Relationships of all types may begin based on shared interests, mutual attraction and linked outlooks. But outside of Eden, they need additional fuel to keep them thriving.

The cherubs reveal that there is no energy source for building relationships comparable to that which results from jointly studying God's word.

Instead of frantically seeking crowds of friends, build spiritual compatibility with a chosen few. Sharing how your day went with a spouse, child, grandchild or friend is valuable; but whether you are in one location or across the continent from each other, be sure to discuss ideas and values as well. Superficial relationships breed loneliness; our souls crave more.

WAIT TILL YOU HEAR THIS!

Gossip isn't slander, right?

Have you seen the latest episode of *Gossip Girl*? Read *National Enquirer* lately? How about *People Magazine*? Decrying gossip may seem quaint today, but with over one hundred magazines, TV shows and websites selling gossip, maybe we ought to remind ourselves of its dark side.

The more we value something the more specific we are in discussing it. For instance, to me, flour is just flour. However, if I'm shopping for my wife I am forced to differentiate between unbleached, bread, whole wheat and various other types.

The Bible contains many different words for ways to communicate because it places such high value on human connection. These words are not interchangeable; each has a specific meaning.

Leviticus 19:16 is commonly translated as:

Do not go about spreading slander among your people...

The Hebrew literally reads as:

Do not peddle gossip among your people...

Everyone agrees that slander is destructive and Biblical laws prohibiting it spawned similar civil laws. But gossip isn't slander, right? Gossip is neutral and harmless, isn't it?

Unlike any other language, Hebrew words magically intertwine with one another in a mystical dance. Every word in the Bible sends the student on a search for words that share the same roots and letters. Thus we get a clue to gossip's essence by noting that the Hebrew for gossip, R-CH-L also means peddler. Ancient Jewish wisdom tells us that both these words also relate to R-G-L, the root word for spying.

In other words, gossiping, peddling and spying are closely related ideas.

This helps us understand the reference to "peddle" in Leviticus 19:16. Peddlers convey goods from one person to another just as spies carry information. Similarly, gossips transmit details about one person to another. Peddlers provide economic benefit while spies can be either heroes or villains depending on your loyalties. Think Nathan Hale vs. Benedict Arnold.

What about the gossip? The prohibition in Leviticus seems to suggest it is always evil. But how do we define gossip? After all, if we never talk about other people, we might never discover someone needing our help. We could become utterly alienated from our families and communities.

What turns positive communication into negative gossip?

The Hebrew reveals the answer. While earning his living, a peddler does benefit his customer by selling him a desired product at a fair price. The patriotic spy engages in dangerous clandestine surveillance in order to help his country, but we have contempt for the amoral spy who engages in his activity for self-enrichment.

So here is the foolproof monitoring system you need to install somewhere between your brain and mouth. Before speaking about another person, ask yourself, "Who am I trying to benefit?" If your answer is "me," you can be sure you are about to gossip.

Perhaps you want to fill an awkward silence, or perhaps you want to draw attention to yourself and appear important. Either way, if you breach a confidence or invade someone's privacy, you are crossing the line from communication into gossip.

The gossiper always finds an audience but all recognize that he is not someone in whom to confide. Gossiping reduces you in the eyes of others.

Gossip shatters relationships. The victim often discovers who spoke about him and then shuns that person forever.

Third, listening to gossip not only coats you with a slimy, subconscious sense of reduced worth but it forever changes your opinion of the person under discussion.

Decrying gossip is far from outdated. It is one of the most important self-improvement steps you can undertake. Banning gossip at your family's dinner table and making your workplace a gossip-free-zone, will improve productivity in both arenas.

19

ARE YOU A TWENTY OR AN EIGHTY?

Life in Egypt certainly wasn't pleasant for the Israelites yet eighty percent of them refused the chance to leave.

My wife owns many cook books. We both enjoy those colorful volumes, each detailing dozens of mouth watering recipes. In an idle moment the other day, I estimated that one shelf alone contained about a thousand recipes. I couldn't restrain myself from the next calculation: I figured out that I had tasted only about two hundred of those dishes.

If you enjoy cooking or baking, you also probably use about 20% of your recipes 80% of the time. You probably wear about 20% of your clothing 80% of the time. Perhaps about 80% of your social connectivity comes from interactions with only 20% of your friends. There are plenty of examples of the famous eighty-twenty rule attributed to Italian economist, Vilfredo Pareto.

If you are in sales you already know that about 80% of your sales revenue comes from 20% of your customers. Successful sales professionals try to replace less valuable customers with more profitable ones.

It is less of a mathematical rule and more an observation that most of our important results come from a small part of our effort. Another variation is that about 20% of the people in any society or community are exceptional and stand out. Perhaps 80% of the good work and charitable endeavors in your town are performed by 20% of the citizens. Likewise, another 20% of the citizens perpetrate about 80% of the crime and destructiveness.

I first learned of this rule when I was nine years old. It was a few weeks before Passover and my father, the late Rabbi A.H. Lapin, was teaching me the book of Exodus. Here is the relevant verse.

> *...and the Children of Israel went up*
> *<u>armed</u> out of Egypt.*
> (Exodus 13:18)

Now the word "armed" in that verse is one possible translation for the Hebrew word which is "CHaMuSHiM" but if you have already gained a glimpse into the majesty and mystery of the Lord's language in my book *Buried Treasure*, you know that Hebrew words in Scripture possess several layers of meaning.

You can easily see here that this word "CHaMuSHiM" shares the same root letters as the word for the number five, CHaMeSH.

חמשים
armed

חמש
5

Ancient Jewish wisdom offers an additional meaning to the above verse. Instead of only reading the word CHaMuSHiM as 'armed' we must also read it as the fraction one fifth. This informs us that given the opportunity to leave Egypt with Moses, in fact only 1/5 or 20% of the nation chose to do so. Astounding!

What a shocker! Life in Egypt certainly wasn't pleasant for the Israelites yet eighty percent of them refused the chance to leave. The truth is that like the Israelites, most of us eventually become accustomed to our existence no matter how painful. We often prefer just to suffer our hardships rather than face the fear of risking the unknown when we try to change our lives for the better. Heading off into the desert with Moses was just plain scary. Eighty percent of the Israelites dismissed him as a dangerous crank.

In the 18th century only a minority of Americans were ready to fight for independence from King George. Life under England certainly wasn't pleasant but 70% of Americans preferred it to facing the fearful unknown of war. We owe our independence to a group of people who were a small and often derided minority.

Times are now challenging. It is easy to feel as if external pressures are dictating our lives leaving us passive and paralyzed in a powerful parallel to being in our own Egypt.

80% of people resignedly adjust to living permanently in their predicaments, but you can be among the 20% who reject an unacceptable reality and boldly build a bridge to better times. It does require considering steps that most people would reject. It does require facing down your fears.

20

HEY BUDDY, GOT A LIGHT?

Staying the same is an illusion,
not reality.

W hat three changes could you institute that would improve your life? Most people know exactly what they ought to do and what they ought to stop doing that would make their lives better. Which begs the question; why don't we just go ahead and do these things?

The answer is what I call "The Force of Darkness." Understanding and learning to conquer this sinister force is so important that God introduces us to this primeval darkness and general chaos no later than the second verse of Genesis.

According to ancient Jewish wisdom this verse reveals a dark force built into the universe that attempts to combat progress towards improving our lives. This is why it is harder to diet, exercise and grow thin, than it is to sit around, eat and grow fat. This is why it is harder to save and invest than it is to spend and consume or to educate one's self and improve one's career rather than to seek entertainment. This is why self-discipline is harder than indulgence or why it is harder to build a marriage than it is to destroy one. In other words, keeping the flame burning is just plain hard. It is far easier to sit back and allow darkness to win.

If the problem is darkness, surely the antidote is light – which brings us to Chanukah, the festival of light.

Many mistakenly think that Chanukah is a post-Biblical rabbinical holiday. Nothing could be further from the truth. In fact, its roots lie in the Torah and within the prophecies of Hagai and Zecharia, centuries before the historic events.

Many mistakenly think that Chanukah exists because about 2,150 years ago the Hasmonean Maccabees won an extraordinary military victory over the Greeks and Jewish Hellenists. Nothing could be further from the truth. In fact, one of the reasons the loyal and faithful Jews were able to win the war was because it was fought on the days already prophetically preordained for light to defeat darkness.

Many mistakenly think that Chanukah is an annual holiday celebrated by playing silly games while eating oily potato latkes. Nothing could be further from the truth. In fact, just as ranchers must vaccinate their livestock each year to keep them healthy, Chanukah is an annual vaccination of light to keep ourselves healthy enough to dispel darkness.

On the first night of Chanukah we light one flame. We add a flame each successive night until we have a glorious extravaganza of light emanating from our menorah on the eighth night. Why don't we increase the total light on this holiday by kindling eight flames every night?

Simple arithmetic reveals that lighting correctly requires a total of 36 flames. It is no coincidence that the word light appears 36 times in the Torah. It is also no coincidence that the first word in the Bible possessing the numerical value of 36. is the Hebrew word meaning "Where are you?" which God asks Adam after his sin. You see, in Hebrew, each letter has a numerical value and the four letters of that word have the values of 1; 10; 20; and 5 for a total of 36.

Needless to say, God knows where Adam is hiding. The question was not an attempt to discover Adam's physical whereabouts but instead it was God admonishing Adam to reflect on his spiritual condition.

That word echoes down the ages as God asks each one of us every day, "Where are you?" The message of the 36 bright flames, increasing by one each night, is that you dispel darkness by achieving just a bit more today than you did yesterday. Remaining in one place is just a slower way of moving in the wrong direction. Staying the same is an illusion, not reality. That is simply the way God created the world.

21

PSSST! WANT TO BECOME FAMOUS?

Building things up takes more time and effort than breaking them down.

W hat regular daily activity did Ronald Reagan, Winston Churchill, Harry Truman and General George Patton all share? The answer is that, along with many other distinguished men and women, these leaders all kept diaries.

If you consider it a coincidence that many famous people happen to have kept diaries, you'd be wrong. It is not that eminent personalities keep diaries. It is that ordinary people who keep diaries often become notable. All the diarists listed above started keeping diaries long before they became famous.

Let me explain with a nugget of ancient Jewish wisdom.

Upon leaving Egypt, the Israelites were directed to count formally each passing day for seven entire weeks until the fiftieth day which would be the holyday of Shavuot or Pentecost. This is the day on which God gave Moses the Ten Commandments on Mount Sinai. (Leviticus 23:15-16) Thus, fifty days after acquiring physical freedom, they would acquire spiritual freedom by accepting God's message to mankind, the Torah.

People often mistakenly assume that their counting reflected their eagerness to reach Mount Sinai and receive the Torah. However, had this been so, the counting would be in descending order, just the way school children count down to summer vacation. On the day after the Exodus, they would have said "Today there are 49 days left," and thus day by day they would have counted down to zero. In reality, the Israelites counted in ascending order, starting with one and ending with forty-nine on the eve of Shavuot, just as we do today.

There can be only one explanation and ancient Jewish wisdom confirms it. We are not counting how many days remain; we are counting how many have passed. The seven weeks separating Passover and Shavuot are meant to be 49 days of spiritual growth and the first step in authentic self-development is to recognize the passage of time and the value of each and every day. There is no better way to do this than engage in a formalized daily ritual that marks each passing day.

In Judaism, the days of the week are numbered not named. Sunday is day one, Monday is day two, and so on. In the Torah, the months are also numbered rather than named. These are further examples of the stress placed on keeping ourselves aware of time's passage.

Through old French and Latin, both the words "journal" and "diary" are derived from the word day. Even the word "journalist" used to apply to someone who wrote for a daily newspaper. It follows that the entire purpose of a diary or a personal journal is to record things on a daily basis.

Most of us would take no more than ten seconds to think of three actions we could take that would utterly ruin our lives. What is more, each of those three ways to destruction could be accomplished in just a few hours, at most. However, if I asked you to think of three things you could undertake that would significantly improve your life, it would be much harder, wouldn't it? What is more, once you did think of three life-enhancing actions, you'd notice that all of them would take considerable time and require long-term commitment.

That is one of the permanent principles of ancient Jewish wisdom: building things up takes more time and effort than breaking them down.

Well, one of the most valuable actions you could undertake to enhance your life dramatically is to start keeping a daily journal and adhere to the discipline meticulously. Each evening without fail, on a computer or on a pad of paper, write down the date and record a few lines or paragraphs describing your reactions to things you experienced and things you yourself said or did that day. Remember, it is private so write naturally and honestly and don't be afraid to be self-critical or self-congratulatory. Therein lies the path to real growth.

Keeping a diary will not change your life overnight, but it most certainly will change it. It is not that those who become well-known just happen to keep diaries; it is that those who review their daily actions and keep aware of the importance of each day often deserve to become well-known.

WHY I LEAVE THE CHEESE OFF THAT BURGER

The great mystery of death can easily overwhelm our lives.

Two of the most common misperceptions about Judaism are that kosher food means food that has been blessed by a rabbi and that Judaism does not believe in an afterlife.

One of the reasons so many Jews mistakenly assume that their faith ignores existence after death is because the Hebrew Bible, known as the TaNaCH, contains so few references to what happens after death.

Indeed, throughout the Torah God promises those who live by the Covenant a good life in this world rather than rewards in the world to come. In spite of its importance, there is a reason for this paucity of information on the afterlife. Though we know it is there, and we need to know that in the world to come we will be called to account for our actions in this world, focusing on the afterlife is just counterproductive.

The reason is simply that the great mystery of death can easily overwhelm our lives, utterly robbing us of passion and spontaneity. Death, the shocking gateway to the unknown, can infect our very essence, coloring our souls with a compelling but subconscious negativity. In some faiths, allowing death to become an obsession makes people contemptuous of life and diminishes the value of their own lives as well as the lives of others.

Thus Jews are urged to avoid all unnecessary contact with death. Séances or other gatherings intended to 'raise the dead' are prohibited. In no way does Scripture suggest that communicating with the dead is impossible, just that it's a really bad idea.

Obviously people do die and we mourn. However the mourning is not for the departed. Safe in the arms of our Father in Heaven, they are fine. It is we who are impacted by the death and it is for our loss that we mourn. One purpose of mourning is to go through a formal process that helps banish the aura of death, allowing us to return to our normal exuberant love of life.

Being subconsciously but overwhelmingly aware of death inhibits us from rapturously embracing life. It interferes with staying happy and diminishes our ability to plan our lives and live our plans.

The seductiveness of death is clear to anyone who has slowly driven past an accident scene, peering at someone lying on the ground. It is equally clear to anyone who has sat in a darkened room watching a movie displaying people getting killed. Death exerts a fatal fascination while, at the same time, it subtly disrupts life in ways we don't always recognize.

In an effort to separate our day-to-day lives from the oppressive and paralyzing impact of death, the Torah commands

Jews to separate 'death food' and 'life food.' Meat is viewed as a perfectly legitimate food for humans but we have to realize that an animal yielded its life to provide that hamburger. On the other hand, milk is the food of life. No animal died in order to provide it and furthermore, milk is the first nourishment all baby mammals encounter.

Both meat and dairy products are recommended foods in Judaism and indeed both have important ritual roles. However, as part of the laws of kosher food, meat and dairy are kept quite separate in Jewish cooking.

Ancient Jewish wisdom points out that the following prohibition appears three times in the Bible.

> *Do not cook a goat in its mother's milk.*
> (Exodus 23:19, 34:26, Deuteronomy 14:21)

Scripture doesn't waste our time with arcane commandments. Who would have thought of cooking a goat in its mother's milk? In addition, there is not one superfluous letter in the Bible. Repetitions are there to teach something new.

The emphasis on this passage is meant to reveal the cosmic truth that there is a deep gulf between meat and milk, which is to say, between life and death.

As humans we experience both but we need to keep them separate. Allowing the spirit of death to intrude can rob our lives of their full potential. While Jews should avoid eating meat and dairy foods together, all who wish to enhance their lives can choose to block obtrusive images of death in entertainment or the news and recognize them as a form of spiritual pollution.

THREE CHEERS FOR FEARS

***
**The Jewish people owe the Egyptian a courtesy!
How can that be?**

When times are tough our mood seems to be more nervous apprehension than eager anticipation. A vague sense of disquiet permeates our lives.

Maybe, just maybe, that could be a good thing.

Ancient Jewish wisdom teaches that the physical realities of the world in which we live provide vital clues to spiritual realities. For instance, internal and external locations of the reproductive organs of both sexes reveal important distinctions between the spiritual nature of men and women.

This is why we should not ignore a crucial spiritual clue we gain from an amazing fact about child birth.

Immediately after a baby's birth, doctors perform an assessment of the newborn's health. Medical personnel rate the baby's respiration, heartbeat, appearance and other factors. This is done in order to determine whether any intervention is required.

Now this will amaze you. A baby born by caesarean section is *expected* to score significantly lower than one who arrived through the birth canal!

It should be just the opposite. The natural childbirth process squeezes and pushes the infant in ways that some child welfare activists would outlaw if they could. However, the child born through caesarean section is spared that entire trauma.

The spiritual insight we get from childbirth is that we humans often get stronger from adversity. I hate to quote the slightly bizarre nineteenth century German philosopher *Friedrich Wilhelm Nietzsche* but he did make two interesting observations.

In what has become a well known phrase, he noted, *"That which does not kill us makes us stronger."* Later, recognizing the centuries of persecution and oppression to which European Jews had been subjected, he made an astounding assertion: *"...The Jews, however, are beyond any doubt the strongest, toughest and purest race now living in Europe"* (*Beyond Good and Evil,* 1886) The Jews, says Nietzsche, were strengthened by adversity.

Before Jonas Salk and Albert Sabin developed the polio vaccine in the middle of the twentieth century, the disease was the most dreaded childhood scourge in America. One of its peculiarities was that it struck upper class families disproportionately. Doctors theorized that the tougher, less hygienic existence of poor people offered them a degree of immunity. We see once again that adversity can help to produce strength.

Now bear with me for a moment as we contemplate the horrors of slavery that the Hebrews endured in Egypt. The book of Exodus offers graphic descriptions. They were oppressed and enslaved. Their baby boys were murdered. They were beaten and tortured and their families were decimated.

This makes the following verse utterly incomprehensible.

You shall not abhor the Egyptian because
you were a stranger in his land.

(Deuteronomy 23:8)

Excuse me! We Hebrews did not exactly choose to be a stranger in his land, and while we were there he was a pretty appalling host. Yet we owe the Egyptian a courtesy? How can this be?

Ancient Jewish wisdom provides the answer. Egypt was the womb of the nation of Israel. It was in that tough and harsh environment that a nation grew which later was able to endure the travails of birth – the Exodus. Interestingly enough, the Hebrew word for Egypt – *Mitzrayim* – actually means narrow and constricted passageway, just like a birth canal.

So yes, Jews may not abhor the Egyptian even until today because over three thousand years ago, the Jewish nation was forged within his. He may not have meant well, but he did the Jews a favor nonetheless. He surrounded them with challenge and adversity which forged the strength that would allow them to survive for millennia. An eternal people.

Everyone can picture a man who grew up in utter poverty but eventually became wealthy. He now drives his grandchildren to their school in his limousine. After school he picks them up and gives them money to spend at the mall. Is he doing them a favor?

When times are tough, do not be fearful. Embrace the adversity and cherish the challenge. It can make you stronger and bring you success.

24

NO THANKS TO YOU

**It feels unnatural and rather uncomfortable
to thank someone who was
indifferent to your fate.**

A good friend got fired yesterday. What a devastating experience! Oh, I know there are more polite ways of putting it. There was corporate restructuring. He was downsized. Bottom line – he got fired. And that is never fun. For a man losing a job is more serious than just losing income. It can erode his dignity.

Because I know him well and am familiar with his competence and integrity I assured him that he will soon be employed again. What is more, I promised he will eventually find a far better job and will look back on yesterday as one of the most important days of his professional career. In fact, I said, he'll actually want to seek out his former boss and thank him for letting him go.

Now that is a special category of Thanksgiving, isn't it? Thanking someone who may not have meant you well but whose actions ended up doing you a favor. And therein lies one of ancient Jewish wisdom's secrets about gratitude. Whether you owe someone thanks or not has nothing to do with the other party's intent and everything to do with whether you benefited.

Thanking someone who picks up the keys you dropped comes fairly easily doesn't it? Few of us find it difficult to thank the checker at the supermarket or our taxi driver. But it feels quite unnatural and rather uncomfortable to thank someone who at best was indifferent to your fate but who, nonetheless, unintentionally did you a favor.

It is also difficult to thank the people who are closest to us and who love us and do so much for us. For instance, it sometimes feels awkward to thank a parent or spouse. Which makes doing so all the more important.

"Juden Raus" was the dreaded Nazi yell Jews heard as they were being rounded up for deportation to death camps. It means, "Jews Get Out!" I mention 'Juden" to illustrate the origin of the most common term today for spiritual descendants of Abraham – Jews. The word Jew comes from the anglicized contraction of the name of Jacob's fourth son, Judah.

Judah's mother, Leah, was the first person in the Torah to express gratitude.

> *...and she said, 'This time I will thank God...'*
> (Genesis 29:35)

In Hebrew Judah's name is pronounced YeHuDaH, from the Hebrew root for thanks. Gratitude is such a vital value that although Isaac was the first born Jew and his son, Jacob, had twelve sons, all of Jacob's descendants take their collective name from Judah. It is not hard to see within this name the two letters Y and D which make up the word YaD or hand.

What does hand have to do with gratitude? Do you recognize expressions like, "I really must take this problem in hand," or, "He has a hand in it," and, "He's an excellent handyman?" The word 'hand' is always a metaphor for action.

That is why gratitude and hand are linked through the magic and mystery of Hebrew. Gratitude, in order to count, must be far more than an emotion; it needs an action. At the very least one must verbally express appreciation. A little higher up the moral scale is writing a handwritten note. Still better is sending a gift or doing something in return.

Acting gratefully toward the majority of people is not too hard. Doing so toward people who inadvertently helped you but care nothing for you, or paradoxically toward people who love you, is much harder. The track for moral growth is to do it anyway.

My friend is going to be fine. You know how I am so sure? Because he retained his dignity by thanking his former boss for the years of employment he enjoyed.

THANK GOD FOR JEALOUSY

Esther set the stage to favor her odds.

"Daddy, come here, I need you!" Those words are music to my ears. It doesn't matter how young or old the child, I love hearing that sound. I always have. It makes me feel as if I am living one of the moments for which I was created.

Standing before an audience and conveying some incandescent truth from ancient Jewish wisdom gives me a similar feeling. It was perhaps for this circumstance that I was created. Everyone who is passionately living his or her life has those moments.

Occasionally, while pausing on the threshold of a difficult challenge, trying to decide whether to undertake it or retreat, one hears the little voice demanding, "Was it for this moment and this challenge I was created?" That little voice is echoing a famous phrase from the Book of Esther.

In chapter four, the Jews of Persia seem doomed, and Mordechai implores his niece, Queen Esther, to risk her life by approaching the king. He concludes his entreaty by saying, "Who knows whether it was for just this purpose that you rose to majesty?"

Esther agrees and invites her husband, the king, along with the evil Haman to a private party. They enjoy a pleasant dinner at which the king expresses his affection for Esther by asking if there is anything else she'd like. She invites him to come to yet another private dinner party, once again with Haman as the only other guest. It is at this second gathering that she denounces Haman. Everything hinged on that moment. If the king's friendship and loyalty to his chief of staff, Haman, stood firm, Esther and all the Jews were finished. If she succeeded in driving a wedge between her husband and Haman, all would be well. While Esther knew the outcome was in the hands of God, she also knew that God expects us to do all in our power to help ourselves. What was the importance of these intimate parties?

In fact, Esther was setting the stage to favor her odds. Let me explain –

Imagine some guy challenging a much stronger friend to a competition where they will each move a fifty-gallon drum filled with water a distance of ten feet. Only, he will move his drum from the roof of a house to the ground, while his friend will be required to move the same weight, the same route, but from the ground to the roof. I'd recommend you bet on the man who proposed the competition. It is really unwise to gamble against the physical law of gravity. It is equally unwise to bet against spiritual laws.

Queen Esther knew that God built certain reactions into men concerning women. We were created so that a social unit of two men and one woman is unstable. This is precisely why history reveals many instances of societies managing with polygamous marriages. Though not ideal, one man and two women can function. However, history cannot offer even one example of a successful polyandrous society – where one woman and two men marry. It never has worked and never will.

Esther knew that a social unit of one woman and two men is intrinsically unstable. By inviting only her husband and one more man to an intimate dinner there was a very good chance that she could introduce just enough subconscious jealousy to rouse an emotional, angry reaction in her husband.

Marriage is both a challenging undertaking and one of the activities for which we are created. The Bible is full of insights into the relationship between husbands and wives, and like Esther, the more you know of the reactions that God instilled in us, the more successful you can be. With all the potential difficulties we face today, applying information from the Torah revealing how the world really works helps ensure that we are betting on a winning formula.

26

HE KNEW HER – OR DID HE?

What activity offers human beings the greatest pleasure?

My parents were classical music enthusiasts so I grew up familiar with the works of many of the great composers. Had you asked me, I would have said that I knew Beethoven's Sixth Symphony, the *Pastoral.* Then, a few years back, my son-in-law Max directed me to an audio program in which a wonderful music teacher discussed the piece.

This led me to an "Aha!" moment. I certainly recognized the *Pastoral* and thought I was familiar with it. But after hearing the discussion I realized that I never really did know it until then. Since then, I hear the music with greater appreciation, admiration and humility.

One of the things I love about studying the Bible is that there are continual "Aha!" moments. No matter how many times I study a passage, each reading reveals new and deeper insights. Usually it is the original Hebrew that points me to more profound meaning.

In my book, *Buried Treasure: Secrets for Living from the Lord's Language*, I wrote seven pages explaining the Hebrew word YaDaH, which means "know." Still, I barely scratched the surface of the many life lessons and truths that emerge from that one word.

I demonstrated how the word is composed of two smaller words which translate as "hand" and "eye" thus explaining why self-interest is a prerequisite of knowing. But I ran out of space before being able to ask a really important question: Why would the Bible choose to use the word "know" as a synonym for marital intimacy?

> *Adam knew Eve, his wife, and she conceived*
> *and she bore Cain.*
> (Genesis 4:1)

What activity offers human beings the greatest pleasure? Immature boys (of any age) will respond, "Sex!" The number of sexually active girls who punish themselves through a warped relationship with food or other forms of self-mutilation suggests this isn't so. Boys may initially feel they have found nirvana, but they too eventually find emptiness when physical connection has no emotional commitment. After four decades, the much vaunted sexual revolution has not actually delivered the great happiness it promised.

No, the greatest pleasure available to human beings is getting to know God. Since getting to know God is terribly difficult, and for most of us close to impossible, we resort to the next best alternative: One may obtain an inkling of how thrilling it would be to get to know the Creator Himself by instead getting to know one of His creations, another human being.

I wanted to get to know the Dutch painter, Rembrandt, partially because his closest friend had been a Torah teacher whose books I study; Rabbi Menashe Ben Israel. I spent many hours in the Dutch State Museum studying the old master's paintings. That may not have been quite as satisfying as spending the afternoon with Rembrandt, but it was the next best thing.

Having a spouse allows us truly to know another person. Sex is one, but certainly not the only necessary component of this knowing. Abusing that avenue ends up alienating us, not bringing us closer to each other.

Is the word YaDaH, to know, always used for sex throughout the Bible?

No, it is only used in situations when the man and woman are really building a relationship based on deep inner knowledge of one another. When those qualities are lacking, for instance in a rape, the word "know" is not used.

> *When Shechem...saw her (Dinah),*
> *he took her and <u>lay</u> with her...*
> (Genesis 34:2)

One of my hopes in writing these Thought Tools is that you gain a little of the thrill of knowing God through coming to know a little of His language.

27

THE HAPPY ASTRONAUT

Being happy means practicing a form of spiritual hygiene.

Take this simple quiz:

Does (a) or (b) more accurately describe your emotional state most of the time.

(a) I am happy.

(b) I would be happy if _____
_____. (fill in whatever applies for you)

Our first president's wife, Martha Washington, also took this quiz. Here is how she answered.

> *"I am determined to be cheerful and happy in whatever situation I may find myself. For I have learned that the greater part of our misery or unhappiness is determined not by our circumstance but by our disposition."*

Amazingly, in Deuteronomy chapter 16, God instructs us, "...and you should be only happy." Unlike some of God's directives, whose benefits we don't immediately see, this one seems easy to understand.

For starters, being a happy person means you're practicing spiritual hygiene and refraining from polluting the environment. That makes people enjoy being around you since most folks loathe being around the unpleasant aura of self-indulgent misery. And certainly the general air of well being and bonhomie that emanates from your happy soul impacts your body, making for lower stress and better health. You also remain young looking for longer.

But God does not merely direct us to be happy. Presenting an agonizing list of hideously horrid consequences, in Deuteronomy chapter 28, He informs us why He brings these curses. The first reason is because: "You didn't listen to the voice of the Lord, your God and keep His commandments."

The second is the one that concerns us now: "Because you didn't serve the Lord, your God with happiness and with a glad heart on account of all the abundance."

So, listening to the word of God is a good start but we also had better learn to do so joyously. It is hard to think of any way you could more easily and more immediately impact every area of your life for good than by choosing to be happy – even if at first it takes great effort and even perhaps a little faking. You will see your social life (not to mention your marital life) improve, see your health improve and improve your relationship with God.

Paradoxically, when happiness is your natural state, you are more acutely tuned in to appropriate sadness. Yesterday morning, Dr. David Medved, father of my dear friends, Michael, Jon and Harry, passed away in Jerusalem. But he was much more to me than the father of my friends. He was a dear friend who throughout his life validated every detail of what I am telling you in this Thought Tool.

I met David Medved when he joined the fledgling synagogue that his son Michael and I established near the beach in west Los Angeles. As the most senior member of a synagogue of mostly young Jews rediscovering their heritage, he was often my main resource for wisdom along with fierce and independent leadership. With his courage and intuitive sense of right, more than once he saved my rabbinic skin. But our relationship was also deeply personal.

My wife, Susan, and I asked him to drive us to our wedding reception for no other reason than his warm ebullience was exactly what we wanted to bask in during our marriage celebrations. From then onwards, he was a frequent and, on account of how happy he made all in his company feel, a very welcome guest at our Shabbat table until he moved to Jerusalem.

One summer I fulfilled my dream of sailing under the Golden Gate Bridge. I invited five friends from my synagogue to help me crew my small sailboat up the California coast from its home port in Marina del Rey to the San Francisco Bay. Though he was almost double the age of the other fellows, Dr. Medved was the toughest, most reliable and most fun-loving man on that rough, coastal jaunt. Over the ensuing years, his rollicking recounting of that boisterous trip, including his unplanned leap overboard, brought joy to every audience.

Fueled by his happiness, to his final days he was an indefatigable hiker. With his youthful good looks and physical vitality, he was a perfect match for the ancient Judean Hills around his Jerusalem home.

David Medved was a brilliant physicist who had been part of an early NASA astronaut training program. After joining our young synagogue he quickly became a committed Jew and a serious Bible scholar. Only a few years ago he authored a remarkable book on science and the Bible. He was a business professional, an engineer, an accomplished public speaker and a Jewish leader of renown. He was a devoted father to his four remarkable sons, a loving father-in-law and grandfather. But above all, he radiated a constant love of life, and his ever-present thousand kilowatt smile brought happiness to all who knew him.

In the words of the traditional condolence formula used for millennia, may the All Present One comfort you, Michael, Jon, Ben and Harry, among the other mourners of Zion and Jerusalem.

28

STAR STRUCK

Should you be sand or star?

I bumped into Maria Shriver – literally. I was entering the office of a New York publisher just as she was leaving. I apologized, we wisecracked for about ninety seconds and she was gone. I told quite a few people about it. Then a sobering thought struck me. I'm certain she did not mention our encounter to a single soul. That would be because she is a star and I'm as obscure as a grain of sand.

Ancient Jewish wisdom contrasts a star to a grain of sand or speck of dust. Stars are inexhaustible sources of light and energy; sand and dust only find their significance when they cling to many other tiny particles and become, say, a mighty dam.

In Genesis 13:16, God promises Abraham that his descendants will be numerous as the dust of the earth.

In Genesis 15:5, He promises Abraham that his descendants will be numerous as the stars.

Soon after, we find this promise:

> *...I will greatly increase your offspring*
> *like the stars of the heavens and*
> *like the sand on the seashore...*
> (Genesis 22:17)

Why use both sand and stars? Either would illustrate large numbers. While there is endless *quantity* of both stars and sand, Scripture is also emphasizing *quality*.

Life requires us to view ourselves simultaneously in two contradictory ways. Just as each star is its own world, we each have our own unique individual purpose, separate from those around us. But, only by humbly recognizing that our single existence is as meaningless in the grand scheme as one grain of sand, can we fully realize our star power, shining and beaming energy to those around us.

We sometimes forget the sand message and dream of stardom. Wouldn't it be nice if I could stand out as the star of my company or group of friends?

Well, no, actually it wouldn't.

A star without sand is often an impediment to teamwork. For many years the Seattle Mariners were a rather lackluster team in spite of having enjoyed the services of baseball stars like Randy Johnson, Ken Griffey Jr. and Alex Rodriguez. When they lost those three stars, the Mariners enjoyed a season such as they had never before experienced. They did this without a single star, just a team of good, solid players working together.

When the St. Louis Browns' few stars were off fighting in 1944, the Browns went to the World Series. The Yankees won three world championships in a row without one single big-name baseball star on the team after losing their stars to the war effort. Between them, Mark McGwire and Sammy Sousa hit 136 home runs. They were stars, but neither of their teams amounted to much.

Although fans were gloomy when Wayne Gretzky departed the Edmonton Oilers, that hockey team improved rather than faltered.

Think about jobs you have had. Remember the star? Does anyone think of him fondly? Stars don't do very much for teams. But neither do people who think they are so insignificant that they have nothing to offer.

Accentuating or ignoring our own value may give us a momentary high or make us feel noble, but both are soon followed by a sense of meaninglessness. We thrive when we balance star and sand. Meeting Maria Shriver reminded me of that Torah lesson. And this is the last you'll ever hear from me about meeting that beautiful star.

$UCCESSFUL $PIRITUAL PARENTING

People often drive their children
to fulfill their own ambitions.

D ave had a fifteen year old son who dreamed of becoming a firefighter. Driven by the vision of his child taking over his law practice, Dave forcefully encouraged him to join the debate team, focus on academics and eventually get his law degree. His son did so and joined his father's firm. He did fine, but always regretted not following his passion.

For some parents it's academics, for others sports. People often drive their children to fulfill their own ambitions or force their children onto paths intended to enhance their own social aspirations. Far too many parents don't listen to the child's soft voice trying to find expression.

Living our life through our child while remaining indifferent to his unique qualities is not right. God granted us the privilege of nurturing one of His children to adulthood. Part of the thrill of parenting is learning to know that little person and gradually guiding that child to achieve full potential in whatever he or she was created to do.

Come along with me as we visit Joseph, serving as viceroy of Egypt. He brings his two sons to his aged father, Jacob or Israel, for a final blessing.

> *And Joseph took the two of them, Ephraim with*
> *his right hand to the left of Israel, and Menashe*
> *with his left hand to the right of Israel, and he*
> *drew close to him. And Israel extended his right*
> *hand and placed it on Ephraim's head though*
> *he was the younger son, and his left hand upon*
> *the head of Menashe; he crossed his hands*
> *though Menashe was the first-born.*
>
> (Genesis 48: 13-14)

Why did Jacob cross his hands? Clearly, he wanted to give the right-hand blessing, usually reserved for the older son, to the younger Ephraim, but quite understandably, Joseph had placed Menashe, the older, in front of Jacob's right hand.

Why didn't Jacob say, "Boys, would you mind switching places?" Alternatively, he could have accomplished the same thing by gently pushing the boys to change position. But no, he crossed his hands. This isn't an easy feat for a 147-year-old man.

Let me tell you why he chose to achieve his goal this way. Moving the boys would have meant manipulating his grandchildren for his own purpose. You see, Jacob knew that it was up to him to do what was needed rather than involve his grandsons in his stage-managing.

Jacob viewed his two grandsons in the context of future history. Ancient Jewish wisdom records that he saw them as the key to eternal blessing. Indeed he concludes with these words:

And he blessed them that day, saying:
Through you shall Israel bless (their children) saying,
'May God make you like Ephraim and as Menashe,'
and he placed Ephraim before Menashe.

(Genesis 48:20)

And those words are exactly how we bless our sons each Sabbath. (There is a separate blessing for daughters, but that is a subject for another Thought Tool).

Jacob knew that Ephraim, the younger, represented spiritual mastery while Menashe represented materialistic achievement. Both are important. Connecting with God and earning a living are the two concerns that most parents have for their sons. While each child needs both the Ephraim and the Menashe blessings, Jacob's question was which comes first, as represented by the right hand. He knew that although both blessing are necessary, he needed to emphasize spiritual strength and elevate it above material success.

Spiritual achievement can easily bring material success in its wake; however the reverse is seldom seen.

If you have things <u>you</u> want to do, be like Jacob – do them. Don't force your children to do them for you. But doing everything in our power to inject spiritual mastery into our children's souls is very worthwhile. Once they are on that path, ensuring that they possess the ability to make a living is also a vital parenting function. Both these need to be accomplished without forcing our children into activities that reflect our dreams, not theirs.

30

UP THE DOWN STAIRCASE

What can you do when you're heading down?

Man on Wire is the title of a 2008 movie documenting Philippe Petit's 1974 high wire walk between the twin towers of the World Trade Center, a quarter of a mile above the streets of Manhattan. The movie enchanted me. More importantly however, the film maker's camera revealed a truly vital life lesson. During the entire forty-five minute stunt, I never once saw Philippe look down.

This really resonated with me because when I first learned to ride a motorcycle, my instructor insisted that when going into a curve, "Fix your eyes on the end of the turn." Focus your eyes on where you want to go because where you look is where you will end up.

Well, I seldom ride motorcycles anymore and I never walk a tight rope but many times each day I do have the opportunity of focusing my vision on the destination I wish to reach. I am sure you do too.

In real life, we cannot always control our destiny. Things happen. However we can control whether we view those events as ladders or chutes. If we view them with downcast eyes we tend to follow our vision down the chute. But if we lift our eyes upward and view the event as a ladder, it tends to become one.

This is why we read in Scripture the frequent phrase, "...lifted up his eyes," just as we see in this verse:

> *On the third day Abraham lifted up his eyes*
> *and saw the place from the distance.*
> (Genesis 22:4)

On this most confusing mission of his life, Abraham thought he was on his way to sacrifice his beloved son Isaac on Mount Moriah. The sight of his destination must have filled his heart with sadness. He was following God's directive which was leading to great pain. Then Abraham forced himself to raise his vision. Abraham followed this important secret of ancient Jewish wisdom: Lift up your eyes. As difficult as it is, view your next step as an ascent and it will become one. Instead of ending with unbearable grief, Abraham's day concluded in glory.

There are many life occurrences that people perceive as rungs in a ladder leading up to better times. Relieved students celebrate graduations and happy couples celebrate engagements and marriages.

However, other things happen too. Romances break up. Marriages struggle for survival. Interviews fail to turn into offers and jobs are lost. Worrying health issues and economic difficulties can exacerbate family tensions.

These are much harder to view as ladders leading to new opportunities but a verse in Exodus can help. Remember that each and every Hebrew word in the Bible has hidden layers of deep meaning.

The last verse of chapter 20 in Exodus is often translated in English like this:

Don't go up by steps to my altar...

The English conceals something important. In Hebrew, the word for "steps" is "Ma'ALoT." The root of that word means "ascend" or "go up." Indeed, fifteen of the Psalms (120–134) are known as the Songs of Ascent, opening with exactly that word for step – Ma'ALoT.

Of course, in reality, steps are bi-directional; one uses them either to go up or down. And here is why this Hebrew word combines "step" and "ascend." Even when we are forced to take a step down, we must view it as a potential ascent. If we see steps as "ma'alot," an opportunity for ascent, keeping our eye on the goal just as surely as Philippe Petit did, we can lift our eyes and follow with our bodies.

Listen to King David practice this advice.

A Song of Ascent, from out of the depths
I call out to you, Oh Lord...
(Psalms 130:1)

From the depths of misery, David clearly identifies himself as moving upwards. We would do well to follow his lead.

31

WART DID YOU SAY?

We do have such a 'landlord.'
We call it our soul.

D r. Lewis Thomas served both as Dean of Yale Medical
School and president of the world famous cancer
hospital, Memorial Sloan-Kettering Institute in New York.
This extraordinary doctor wrote a beautiful essay describing
a medical test wherein a group of patients suffering from
multiple warts was hypnotized and the people were told that
the warts on the left sides of their bodies would go away
while the warts on the right would remain. Sure enough,
within a couple of weeks virtually all the patients had lost
the warts on the left sides of their bodies with no change
on the right. The few exceptions were people who had difficulty distinguishing their right from their left.

Astounded by this and other similar tests, Dr. Thomas
concluded that we have inside of ourselves something in
charge of our bodies. In his words:

> *"...a Person in charge, running matters of*
> *meticulous detail beyond anyone's comprehension,*
> *a skilled engineer and manager, a chief executive officer,*
> *the head of the whole place. I never thought before that I*

possessed such a tenant. Or perhaps more accurately,
such a landlord, since I would be, if this is in fact
the situation, nothing more than a lodger."
(*The Medusa and the Snail*, Lewis Thomas, Viking Press. 1979)

Of course he is right. Indeed we do have such a "landlord." We call it our soul. Lewis Thomas was not the only eminent medical specialist who, by reaching the very pinnacle of his profession found himself face-to-face with spiritual mysteries.

The winner of the 1963 Nobel Prize in Medicine, Sir John Eccles was a professor at both the Chicago Institute for Biomedical Research and the medical school at the University of Buffalo. He wrote that medical research brings one, "to the religious concept of the soul and its special creation by God." He goes on to say –

"I believe that there is a fundamental mystery in my existence, transcending any biological account of the development of my body, including my brain..."
(*Facing Reality*, Sir John Eccles, Heidelberg Science Library. 1970)

Many smart, educated people, possessing both intellectual honesty and humility, reject a purely materialistic explanation for our human existence. We are both body and soul. We have physical bodies with physical needs and we also have spiritual souls with spiritual needs. Ancient Jewish wisdom teaches that rather than thinking of myself as a body that has a soul, I should really see myself as a soul that currently inhabits a body.

To be sure, our bodies require tangible, physical commodities like air, water and food. However, that isn't enough. We need more because those basic necessities of biological life do nothing for our souls.

For instance, we need the love and esteem of other people. That's a spiritual need in that we can't measure it as we can calorie or oxygen input. No doctor will predict death for friendless people. Likewise, we have a need for accomplishment. Without knowing that we are achieving growth and that by tomorrow, in some area, we will be more than we were yesterday, our souls shrivel up. Similarly, we need to be givers. Theoretically, our bodies can thrive if we are only takers; but our souls cannot. Without giving to others, our souls shrivel up.

In some mystical way that confounds those who see only a physical world, people with no social life, no sense of accomplishment and who take but don't give, do not thrive physically either. It is actually even more important to take care of our souls than our bodies because it is feasible for a sick body to contain a healthy and vibrant soul, but the reverse is quite impossible.

Humanity's attempt to ignore its spiritual needs go way back. This was the core of the battle between Abraham and Nimrod, the architect of the Tower of Babel.

As Abraham understood, just as we try to supply our bodies with all they need to function healthily, we would be well advised to do the same for our souls. That way, our souls will be equipped to do far more for the quality of our lives than merely removing warts.

32

FIRE! AIM! READY!

Temerity usually triumphs over timidity.

Have you ever watched a mother trying to cajole her boisterous youngster into bedtime? Her hesitant tone of voice telegraphs a message to her toddler that he only has to hold out a bit longer to get his way.

I have helped train inexperienced sales professionals who approach their prospects with such trepidation that the sale is lost before it begins.

Military campaigns such as the unstoppable German invasion of France through the forests of the Ardennes in May 1940 revealed the same principle – the committed usually conquer the complacent.

Or put another way, determination usually defeats diffidence. Kids are determined not to go to bed; customers are often determined not to buy and the German panzer units were determined to bypass the far larger French army dug in on the obsolete Maginot line.

Whether in the fields of parenting, business development, or military strategy, temerity usually triumphs over timidity.

The holiday of Chanukah provides some valuable insight here. Unlike any other holiday, it is associated with two distinct and separate historical incidents.

During the week when the Chanukah flames flicker to life, Jews recite an ancient prayer thanking God for two separate miracles.

At least three times on each of the eight days of Chanukah we recite prayers thanking God for the miraculous military victory over the Jewish Hellenists and their Greek allies.

Yet the prayers also mention how after the Greeks defiled the Jerusalem temple only one day's worth of pure olive oil was found. Unexpectedly it burned for eight days. We remember that by celebrating Chanukah for those same eight days.

So what is the background of Chanukah? Is it a marvelous military victory or is it miraculous oil burning for eight days? Will the real Chanukah please stand up?

In reality those two events go together. The military victory is really a reflection of the burning flame. With an unquenchable flame of commitment and determination burning in the hearts and minds of the Macabees, their victory against larger and stronger forces was assured.

The quality of light is such that even a small candle can drive back the stygian darkness of a large cellar and a small flashlight can help guide the traveler through a dark forest.

One of the reasons that Jews usually light the Chanukah menorah in a window of their homes is to demonstrate fearlessness in the fulfillment of this religious obligation. Doing so captures the central intent of strengthening our determination and our commitment.

Once we have mastered the importance of courageously lighting the flame of Chanukah, we can expect also to master lighting our own inner flames of boldness and resolve.

33

GIFT-WRAPPED FROM THE HEART

Giving a gift strengthens a bond.

For me, one welcome sight of the holiday season is malls filled with shoppers laden down with gifts for family and friends. This is an incredible tribute to our spirit of love for others.

Giving a gift strengthens a bond; you are saying, "I love you." Additionally, gift giving makes the world a less lonely place. Have you noticed the warm feeling you get about the person to whom you give a gift? Not surprisingly, the Hebrew word for love AHaV is rooted in the Hebrew word for give – HaV.

Giving gifts is a powerful tool for making and mending relationships. There are many people with whom you need to retain relationships for either family reasons or business purposes. There is your brother-in-law, Fred, whom you're not crazy about. That customer Agatha, who makes you jump through hoops but whose business is significant. Wouldn't you like to feel more genuine warmth toward them?

I think the answer should be "Yes!" particularly when you realize that most people possess a subtle sense of whether you really like them or are merely putting on an insincere act. Giving a gift to Fred and Agatha is less about making them feel closer to you and more about making you feel much more warmth toward them.

Notice the gift that Jacob sent with his ten sons to the second most powerful man in the world, Pharaoh's right-hand man.

> *...carry down a present to the man, some oil, and*
> *a little honey, spices, nuts, and almonds*
> (Genesis 43:11)

Why did Jacob dispatch such a seemingly worthless gift to a major political figure?

This question is even more baffling when we recall that Jacob certainly knew how to send lavish gifts. Earlier in his life he sent an enormous gift of livestock to his brother Esau. You can read the extensive list of the five hundred and fifty animals that he sent in Genesis 32:15-16.

Yet to a ruler of Egypt he sent a little party platter?

Jacob knew exactly what he was doing. He knew that his brother Esau was not a sentimental man. Esau was a material- ist who valued life only in material terms, thus for the gift to have impact on both Esau and Jacob it had to be eco- nomically substantive. That gift served as a catalyst for the brothers embracing when they met. (Genesis 33:4) And because Jacob sent a meaningful gift, Esau detected no duplicity in Jacob when they embraced. The gift helped Jacob form a relationship with his estranged brother.

However, when Jacob directed his sons to take a gift to Joseph, he had sensed a clue that Joseph was not focused on money.

At the end of Genesis 32, when Jacob's sons came home from their disastrous food-buying trip to Egypt, each man found his money tucked into his bags of provisions. They were terrified that they were being set up as thieves but their father saw something else. While he didn't know that the ruler of Egypt was his long-lost son, Joseph, he did sense that he was saying, "I don't want your money – I want your love and friendship."

For this reason, he advised his sons to take a personal rather than expensive present with them on their second purchasing expedition. He was not trying to buy Joseph's favor as much as he was trying to transform the emotions that his sons felt toward the Egyptian viceroy. Jacob felt confident that once the ruler detected warmth from the brothers, he would soften. There was no better way to bring this new warmth into the hearts of his sons than have them bring a present of sentimental value.

So as you unwrap those packages this year, remember that each gift sings to you of new and stronger affections felt toward you by the giver.

34

SCHOONERS, YAWLS AND SLOOPS

Which ship will you board?

I am spoiled. When I contemplate boating, I picture vacationing with my family among the magnificent islands of the Pacific Northwest. But except for a blessed few people and times, boarding a ship has not meant leisure, but instead was a risky way for crossing oceans.

Traveling by ship was dangerous and frightening in the days before Carnival Cruises. Ships served as the precarious means of transportation to start a new life, for trade or as a means of livelihood like the potentially deadly 19th century whaling ships and indeed, today's commercial fishing boats.

The book of Jonah opens with a different type of boating:

> *And Jonah arose to flee... from before God...*
> *and he found a <u>ship</u> going to Tarshish...*
> (Jonah 1:3)

> *And God sent a big wind over the ocean and*
> *there was a great storm upon the ocean and*
> *the <u>ship</u> appeared likely to shatter.*
> (Jonah 1:4)

And the sailors were terrified … and they threw
all the articles on the <u>ship</u> into the ocean to make
it lighter and Jonah went down to the bilges
of the <u>ship</u>, lay down and fell asleep.

(Jonah 1:5)

The word ship appears four times in these three consecutive verses. Only by looking at the Hebrew text can you see that the word in the first three instances differs from the fourth. The first three use the the Hebrew word ONiYaH. The final instance of ship uses the word SeFiNaH.

How can Scripture suggest that the ship Jonah slept in is different from the ship described earlier? One clue is that this is the only place in Scripture where a sailing vessel is called a SeFiNaH.

Take a look at two more Biblical vessels. In the days leading up to the great flood, God instructed Noah to make an ark:

Make yourself an <u>ark</u> of gopher wood…

(Genesis 6:14)

Later, Moses' mother floats her son down the Nile:

And when she could hide him no longer
she took for him an <u>ark</u> of bulrushes…

(Exodus 2:3)

Although English translations sometimes call Moses' craft a basket, the Hebrew labels both a TeiVaH.

The different words for floating conveyance reflect different purposes. Neither Noah nor Moses had a destination. Their arks were not designed to be sailed or even controlled. Their boats were merely refuges from peril.

The ship Jonah boards is a commercial one. Her crew chooses to face constant struggle. There might be too much wind or too little. There are shoals and reefs to avoid. The challenging trip is undertaken in order to accomplish a goal.

When Jonah goes to sleep at the end of verse 5, he is using the ship for a uniquely different purpose. He is avoiding reality. The ship is a hiding place for him, not a means to a destination. It isn't even a refuge; he is indifferent to its fate as well as his own.

We get an added clue to the function of a SeFiNaH from the Hebrew word itself. One magic of Hebrew is that certain letters share a relationship. When you exchange one of these letters for the other, the two words that result share a connection. Among these related letters is the first letter of the word for Jonah's boat when he goes to sleep and the first letter of the word for "hidden." (Remember that Hebrew reads from right to left)

צפן
hidden

ספן
(root of) boat

On extremely rare occasions one needs to board an ark. Buffeted by external forces, be they physical, social or economic, there is no further action one can take to influence one's life. At that point finding refuge and surrendering all to God's mercy is the only option.

But most of the time, one wants an ONiYaH, a purposefully sailed ship whose course need to be constantly adjusted and controlled. The ship to avoid at all costs is Jonah's SeFiNaH, the equivalent of burrowing under the blankets and giving up.

In ancient Jewish wisdom, a sailing ship sometimes serves as a metaphor for a self-contained existence. When you leave the dock you must carry everything you need with you. Acquiring anything additional is uncertain; it depends on weather and wind, both of which are out of your control. Preparation is a prerequisite for a successful passage. Part of the preparation is making sure you board the correct ship.

THOUGHT TOOL

35

DANCING WITH THE SNAKES

Do we stride purposefully or saunter languidly?

I did not participate in the hysterical outpouring of emotion
and mass mourning for Michael Jackson. I think he was a
terribly tragic figure who lived a lonely life and died a lonely
death. But he certainly could dance.

His famous 'moon-dance' was magical. Smooth and seductive, it was hard to tear your gaze away; deceptively simple
but almost impossible to replicate. And it wasn't just Michael
Jackson's feet. He carried off the stunning illusion of moving
backwards while walking forward by employing his entire
body. His posture, the tilt of his head and the swing of his
arms were just as important as his fancy footwork.

One doesn't have to admire everything about a man in order
to learn something valuable from him. How we carry our
bodies is important. Do we sit or slouch? Do we stand or
stoop? Do we stride purposefully or saunter languidly? These
things impact our mood and our effectiveness.

If your drill sergeant yelled, "Stand up straight!" he probably
attended the same drill sergeant school as my mother. You
cannot possibly feel alert, let alone look it, while slouching.
You will undoubtedly irritate your boss as you amble leisurely

down the hallway in response to his summons.

Gazing downwards not only makes you look guilty, it also depresses your mood. Conversely standing erect and keeping your eyes above the horizontal prepares you to tackle challenges. Lifting your eyes even higher, until you are looking heavenwards, can increase your feeling of spirituality and enhance closeness with the Creator. Are we humans perhaps created to be able to look at the sky? Doing so is, after all, far easier for people than for animals.

The children of Israel were encouraged to look upwards in a perplexing section of the Bible. After endlessly complaining in the desert, Israel was punished.

> *And God sent, among the nation, snakes which*
> *bit the people and many of the Israelites died.*
> (Numbers 21:6)

The frightened nation atoned and asked Moses to pray for the removal of the snakes.

> *God said to Moses, 'Make a snake and place it*
> *upon a staff. All who were bitten should look up*
> *at the snake and they will live.'*
> (Numbers 21:8)

This, of course is the origin of the well-known medical symbol of healing, the rod of Asclepius, sometimes known as the caduceus.

Ancient Jewish wisdom observes that a snake on a long stick possesses no healing powers. Rather the purpose was to raise the striking image of a copper snake high into the air forcing its viewers to elevate their gazes until they were tilting their necks heavenwards. In that posture the well-known healing power of prayer could get to work.

It might have been with these thoughts in mind that the second president of the United States, John Adams, a devoutly religious man, wrote to his wife, Abigail on July 3rd, 1776.

> *"I am apt to believe that it will be celebrated,*
> *by succeeding generations, as the great*
> *anniversary festival. It ought to be*
> *commemorated, as the Day of Deliverance*
> *by solemn acts of devotion to God Almighty.*
> *It ought to be solemnized with pomp and parade,*
> *with shews (sic), games, sports, guns, bells,*
> *bonfires and illuminations from one end*
> *of this continent to the other*
> *from this time forward forever more."*

'Illuminations' is the word Adams used for what we call fireworks.

Could part of the appeal of fireworks be that they make us gaze heavenwards for extended periods? Perhaps that spiritual high we all feel after a gasp-inducing fireworks display has as much to do with our upwards posture as it does with the virtuosity of the performance.

As military people and moms know, standing erect not only looks good but it energizes us. Gazing upwards feeds energy back into our souls.

36

YOU LOOK FAT IN THAT DRESS

Should you be honest or kind?

Want to live morally? It's easy. Do 'good' things and refrain from 'evil.'

Real life isn't so simple. Most actions contain elements of both good and evil. Sometimes, telling someone the truth causes considerable grief. Is honesty always the best policy?

When your dying parents ask you if they did a great job raising you, you could be honest and retort, "Well, had you supported me instead of always criticizing me I might not have needed eleven years of therapy!" Or is kindness the higher good in which case you smilingly reassure your parents of how grateful you are for all they did.

Your friend proudly shows you the new car he just bought. You know the car received negative reviews and what is more, your friend overpaid. Should you be honest or kind?

Many spouses tell little white lies or withhold information. Wives lie about their dress size or misstate the cost of their hairdressing. Husbands lie about meeting friends for a beer or the cost of their hobbies. Are these spouses behaving badly because honesty is a virtue or are they acting morally because there is value in a peaceful marriage?

So what's a person to do? Study the Bible – that's what!

God didn't give Moses a long list of simple do's and don'ts. The purpose of the entire narrative structure is to throw a laser beam of clarity onto the vast spectrum of human circumstance and challenge. Thousands of pages of ancient Jewish wisdom convey vital information that spring from what seem to be simple stories.

Let's peek into the lives of Abraham and Sarah. In Genesis 18, Sarah overhears an angel telling Abraham that he and Sarah will have a son.

> *And Sarah laughed in herself saying,*
> *'After I have withered will I conceive*
> *– and my husband is old!'*
> (Genesis 18:12)

> *And the Lord said to Abraham,*
> *'Why did Sarah laugh saying:*
> *Shall I truly give birth though I am old?'*
> (Genesis 18:13)

But wait! Sarah clearly mentioned Abraham's age as a factor while God Himself leaves out that humiliating detail.

Ancient Jewish wisdom cites these vital verses in teaching us how to act when there is a truth/kindness clash. God withheld information for the sake of marital harmony. Lying for peace isn't always right, but on occasion it is. Here are some questions to ask ourselves when we are unsure what to say.

1. Will telling the truth harm someone? For instance, imagine you allowed me to stay at your home while I was visiting your town. Upon my return, a pesky neighbor asks me where I stayed. If I tell him that I stayed with you, he'll cadge an invitation and make your life a misery. I am obligated to be evasive in my answer to protect you.

2. Will telling the truth help someone? You purchased some non-returnable item and ask me how I like it. Had my honest evaluation been important, you would have asked me before you committed to the purchase. Now, you are really asking for my affirmation. And that is what you should get.

3. Could my words hurt someone's feelings without achieving any good? Granting a flawed parent peace by not expressing your negative feelings is laudable.

4. Am I going to derive a mean and malicious pleasure out of telling the truth? That is a sure clue that I should zip my lip.

5. When someone in general greeting asks, "What's happening?" this is not an invitation to pass on gossip or bad news no matter how truthfully those responses would answer the question.

6. Am I really hiding my own flaws and my wrong behavior while rationalizing that I am being kind to someone else?

In other words, there are no such things as white lies – only forbidden or permitted speech.

Truth is a virtue. On rare occasion, so is suppressing it.

YOUR MONEY OR YOUR LIFE

How far should we go to defend our property?

In late 2007, 83-year-old Raymond Bunte confronted two young thugs helping themselves to his neighbor, Dolores Hendershot's valuables, out of her suburban San Antonio home. Clutching his shotgun, he blocked their exit and ordered the men to lie down on the ground. They ignored the old-timer and threatened him. He pulled the trigger. One criminal is dead; the other is behind bars.

A few months earlier, just south of Little Rock, 93-year-old Willie Hill woke to find a hoodlum stuffing his pockets with Willie's money, his pocket knife and his hearing aid. 24-year-old Douglas Williams was mighty surprised when Willie reached for his revolver and shot the home invader in the throat.

Finally, in May of that same year, 60-year-old Shirley Reed was about to get into her car outside her apartment in Dallas. 19-year-old Charles Poursoltani suddenly materialized beside her, pointed a gun and demanded the keys to her car. Grandma Shirley declined to comply and instead she wrenched the gun out of her assailant's hand and shot him.

These true stories help us ask how the good Lord wants us to relate to our possessions. Of course we are morally obliged to defend our lives, even with deadly force, but how far should we go to defend our property?

Ancient Jewish wisdom probes the protection of possessions in this verse:

> *If the thief be discovered breaking in and he is*
> *struck and dies, there is no blood guilt.*
> (Exodus 22:1)

Ancient Jewish wisdom explores the nuances of this verse over many pages, but one concept drawn from the verse is that you are not morally obliged to let someone escape with your property.

You originally obtained your possessions honestly. It follows that you used up a certain number of your hours on this earth working to earn enough to pay for that car or that necklace. Now if the thief gets away with your property, you will have to repeat that working time to replace the stolen object. In other words, the thief has deprived you of something far more important than a car or necklace. He has robbed you of time. Since time is the one irreplaceable commodity, he has committed a grievous crime – he has deprived you of some of the time you have left on God's earth.

Here's a question: What is the law if you murder someone so ill that he was guaranteed to die the next day? Can you defend yourself in court by claiming that since you only deprived this elderly man of one day of his life your crime was really insignificant? What if you shot dead, as he plummets past your window on the twentieth floor of the Empire State Building, a man who had committed suicide by jumping off the roof three seconds earlier? Though he was doomed to die seconds after you shot him, you still committed murder.

In other words, stealing even a tiny bit of time from someone's life is terribly serious. Someone who steals your possessions is also stealing time from your life.

I tell you this not to encourage you to shoot a burglar but because the Bible enhances our lives by helping adjust our attitudes until they are more congruent with God's blueprint of reality. We see a similar message in the following verses:

> (Jacob) arose that night, took his two wives,
> his two handmaidens, and his eleven sons,
> and crossed the ford of Jabok. He took them
> and crossed them over the brook along with
> his possessions. And Jacob was left alone
> and a man wrestled with him until sunrise.
> (Genesis 32:23-25)

Ancient Jewish wisdom asks what Jacob was doing alone. The surprising answer is that he was retrieving some small, inexpensive containers of oil.

These verses contain important lessons for us. If we recognize the true cost of each object we purchase, we will be less likely to impulsively buy items that will then sit unused or unappreciated. We are also morally obliged to care for our possessions and avoid losing them because they took time from our lives to acquire.

We should cherish our property. In so doing we can honor God's great gift to us – the days and hours of our lives.

38

RAISE YOUR RIGHT HAND AFTER ME

**In many societies, a new leader is ushered in
over the corpse of his slain rival.**

With only four exceptions in history, American presidents have attended the inaugurations of their successors. There is something both magnanimous and reassuring about this tradition and not surprisingly, given the devotion of early Americans to Scripture, its roots can be found in the Torah.

And the Lord said to Moses:

> *Take for yourself, Joshua the son of Nun,*
> *a man in whom there is spirit,*
> *and rest your hand upon him.*
> (Numbers 27:18)

> *And you shall place some of your majesty upon him...*
> (Numbers 27:20)

> *And Moses did as the Lord commanded him...*
> (Numbers 27:22)

> *And he rested his <u>hands</u> upon him and commanded him...*
> (Numbers 27:23)

Instead of simply declaring Joshua as the new leader to

succeed Moses, God directed Moses to participate in the transfer of power. As the long-time leader, Moses had accumulated goodwill and some majesty, which he was to confer upon his successor. Part of God's blueprint for civilization is the smooth continuity of leadership. When a leader participates in the transfer of leadership to his successor, he helps make this possible.

Ancient Jewish wisdom sheds some light on this piece of practical politics. Did you notice the mention of hands in the verses I quoted?

Let us probe into the mystical meaning of the human hand. Would you agree that when you extend your hand, palm up-wards towards another person, your gesture expresses something like, *"Come here," "I want you/it," or "Give that to me"*?

Now when you reverse your hand, extending your arm with the palm down or away from you, what you are saying is really the reverse – *"Stop,"* or *"No, thank you,"* or *"Enough, no more."*

Here is what the Hebrew word for hand – *YaD* – looks like, just as it is written in a Torah scroll. (Remember, Hebrew reads from right to left.)

יד

hand

Now take a look at the Hebrew word for "enough, no more" pronounced DYe.

די

enough

Astonishingly it is spelled by reversing the Hebrew word for hand.

Reversing our physical hand reverses the meaning of the gesture. Similarly, reversing the Hebrew word for hand reverses its meaning.

When Moses rested his hands palms down on Joshua he was saying the same thing. This is about you. I am taking nothing. I am transferring leadership and offering you whatever goodwill and majesty I have accumulated these past years.

This is why putting your hand on someone's shoulder is usually perceived as a gesture of warmth and empathy.

But wait a moment. God told Moses to rest his hand (singular) upon Joshua but five verses later Moses rested his hands (plural) upon Joshua. Why did Moses take it upon himself to add a hand?

Someone I care about, who badly needed a job, was recently offered a fine position. I asked him what he was going to do. His response – "I am going to grab this opportunity with both hands!" With both hands – meaning with unrestrained enthusiasm.

Ancient Jewish wisdom teaches that God knew that it wasn't easy for Moses to hand over the leadership of Israel. For over forty years Moses had devoted his life to the people. God told Moses, "Go ahead, do it with one hand." I need you to participate in transferring leadership but I understand that there might be an element of sadness and worry. Just do it with one hand.

In response, the great Moses did it with both hands. With boundless enthusiasm and total commitment, Moses transferred leadership to Joshua.

It is magnanimous for a former president to attend the inauguration of his successor though the helicopter waits to carry him away to obscurity. In many societies, a new president is ushered in over the corpse of his slain rival. In successful societies, like America, it is reassuring to see the new president inaugurated in the gracious presence of his predecessor. The Biblical blueprint for civilization brings the blessings of continuity and tranquility.

39

SEEN ANY FALLEN DONKEYS LATELY?

How do we determine the worthiness of a charity recipient?

You've probably heard the joke about the storekeeper who, each Friday afternoon on his way home, dropped a dollar into the cup of the local street beggar. For years, the routine had been the same. The storekeeper greeted the beggar with a cheery, "Hi," dropped his dollar into the beggar's cup and smiled as the beggar's, "Thank you and God bless you" floated behind him.

Times turned bad and one Friday the storekeeper smiled sadly at the beggar and dropped only a quarter into the cup. About to walk on, he was brought to a standstill by an indignant, "Oy!" from the beggar.

"What's the matter with you, why only a quarter?" inquired the incensed tramp.

"Well, times are tough and I've had a bad week," explained the shop owner.

The beggar responded, "And just because you've had a bad week, must I have one too?"

At various time things are a little tougher, sometimes things get a whole lot more difficult. During those times, it is surely a good idea to cut thoughtless spending and random purchases of unnecessary consumer items.

For many of us that can leave a psychic vacuum since spending money does make us feel good – at least until the next monthly bill arrives. So how can we retain the good feelings that spending money causes without actually worsening our financial situation?

Happily, a solution exists. Just make certain that amidst whatever financial anxiety you are feeling, you do not neglect to make your regular charity payments.

When you give a monetary gift to someone who has less than you, this simple action suffuses you with even more good feelings than an hour of indulgence in the local shopping mall. This is because giving money away releases even more dopamine into your brain than shopping does.

Which begs the question of how do we determine the worthiness of a charity recipient? Fortunately, ancient Jewish wisdom comes to the rescue. Try reading this verse from Deuteronomy carefully.

> *You shall not hide yourself if you see your brother's*
> *donkey or ox fallen on the road, instead,*
> *you shall help him right them.*
> (Deuteronomy 22:4)

See that important phrase there? You shall help him right them. Do not do it alone. In other words, if the owner of the fallen animal chooses to sit on the side of the road and watch you trying to repair the situation, you are morally exempt from helping. In fact, you should leave him to his fate. You are doing your brother no favor if you encourage his self-destructive behavior by rescuing him without his taking any steps to help himself.

From this verse, ancient Jewish wisdom teaches that God wants us to help only those who are doing everything possible to help themselves.

President Abraham Lincoln wrote a famous letter to his stepbrother, Johnston, who was again asking for yet another loan of money. In this letter, Lincoln declined to make the loan, observing that his brother did little to help himself.

> *"...You are not lazy, and still you are an idler.*
> *I doubt whether since I saw you, you have done*
> *a good whole day's work, in any one day.*
> *You do not very much dislike to work, and still*
> *you do not work much, merely because it does not*
> *seem to you that you could get much for it.*
> *This habit of uselessly wasting time*
> *is the whole difficulty..."*

However, Abraham Lincoln did make this offer to his sibling. If his stepbrother would take his advice and get a job, for every dollar Johnston earned, his brother Abraham would add another dollar, thus effectively doubling the salary that Johnston earned. History does not record whether Johnston took the president's advice and made good.

In times when it is easier than ever to find people who have less than we do, it is important that we steward our resources responsibly and give our money in a way that really does improve the world. To do so means to follow the Biblical advice and help our brother or sister who are already trying to help themselves.

That way we'll ensure that just because we may be having a harder week, nobody else need have one too. What is more, we'll get the feel-good benefit with no unpleasant surprise lurking in the monthly credit card bill.

40

GRAB A STICK

Surely God could just as easily have performed the miracles of the Exodus without any sticks?

Imagine that in the middle of a detective story you are enjoying, this sentence appears:

> *"The butler entered the library and was horrified to find the body of his master lying motionless in a pool of blood."*

If your eye skipped over that sentence, the rest of the novel would make no sense. Similarly, a software developer would never ignore even one line of code in a complex program. Details matter in mystery novels and in computer software.

Details matter just as much in your Bible study adventures. Allow me to present an example. Early in the book of Exodus, God appears to Moses at the Burning Bush and assigns him the mission of launching the Exodus by returning to Egypt.

Consider these verses:

> *Moses answered, 'What if they do not believe me or listen to me and say, HaShem did not appear to you?'*

Then HaShem said to him, 'What is that
in your hand?' And he said, 'A staff.'

(Exodus 4:1-2)

This introduces us to a stick which becomes quite famous. Yet, surely God could just as easily have performed the miracles of the Exodus without any sticks. Had the entire account never have mentioned a stick, none of us would have inquired, "I wonder why there was no stick in that story?" Still, the stick played a role in many of the plagues and helped to split the Red Sea.

In all these instances, the Hebrew word for this stick or rod is: **MaTeH**.

מטה

There are many other instances of a staff mentioned in Scripture. Here are two examples:

Even though I walk through the darkest valley,
I will fear no evil, for you are with me; your staff
and your rod, they comfort me.

(Psalms 23:4)

Those who spare the staff hate their children,
but those who love them are careful to discipline them.

(Proverbs 13:24)

In these examples, the Hebrew word for the stick or staff is: **SHeVeT**.

Ancient Jewish wisdom emphasizes something important: Both these two Hebrew words, MaTeH and SHeVeT, not only mean sticks but they also mean groups of people and are the two words used for "tribe" as in the twelve tribes of Israel. Thus, in Hebrew, the word for a kind of stick also refers to a group of people.

But wait! The same is true in English isn't it? Staff means a kind of stick but it also means a group of people. For instance, Admiral Michael Mullen is the Chairman of the Joint Chiefs of Staff.

And here is another word for a kind of stick – club. Again, we see a kind of stick which also means a group of people. For instance, "He was denied entry to the exclusive club."

It is fascinating that the words for a stick with which you can beat people are also the words for a gathering of people. Somehow, rooted in the Lord's language, is the idea that a group of people, just like sticks, can inflict injury. Well anyone who has actually been denied entry into a club, or had an organized group of people attack him knows just how hurtful a group of people can sometimes be.

However, the story of Exodus tells us how a stick can work miracles too. The stick of Exodus served as an extension to the arms of Moses and Aaron and punished the Egyptians. It also struck a rock and brought forth water. Just like that stick, a group of people can work miracles too.

When you form friendships and develop groups of people around you, you participate in enormous potential; potential for help and healing but also potential for hurt and harming.

If some aspect of your life seems stalled and you feel the need for a miracle, one important step is get yourself a stick, a club, or a staff. In other words, find a few new friends. Join a group. Do whatever it takes to increase the number of humans you are connected to. And if your group ever seems to turn into a snake, as groups of people can sometimes do, grab that snake and turn it back into something good. Harnessing the power of the group can truly cause miracles to happen.

41

ANGEL ON A MOTORCYCLE

What exactly is an angel?

Have you ever been in a situation where you found yourself calling on your guardian angel? If you've seen active military service, I probably know your answer. Most who have experienced danger answer in the affirmative. This is hardly surprising.

A 2008 Baylor University study showed that more than half of all Americans claim to have been protected from harm by an angel on at least one occasion. They could have attributed their happy escapes to luck or coincidence, but they didn't. They told researchers that they were helped by angels.

But what exactly is an angel? We often use the word, but we mean different things. Some men use the word romantically. Indeed, there are dozens of popular melodies with angel in the title. Some think of angels as delicate creatures with diaphanous wings. Others think of specific angels, like Gabriel.

The Bible frequently speaks of angels without describing exactly what they look like. Furthermore, Scripture is deliberately ambiguous about whether angels are human or supernatural. One can see this clearly in the Hebrew.

Take a look at this verse:

> *And the two <u>angels</u> came to Sodom in the evening*
> *and Lot was sitting at the gate of Sodom.*
> (Genesis 19:1)

Now look at this verse:

> *And the <u>messengers</u> returned to Jacob saying,*
> *'We came to your brother to Esau...'*
> (Genesis 32:6)

The Hebrew word used for "angels" in Genesis 19 and for "messengers" in Genesis 32 is one and the same.

מלאכים
MaLACHiM

That's right – exactly the same word translates as messenger and angel.

Angels are messengers of God. At times they are super-natural; but they can also be humans on a mission. And it makes no difference whether or not those people know that they are acting as messengers of God.

During June and July of 1969, I undertook a grand adventure – a foolhardy motorcycle trip through Africa that surely added gray hairs to my parents' heads. (Note to Lapin children: Do not try this!)

One day I joined a crowd of villagers to watch the Apollo moon landing on the only black and white TV for miles around. It had been wedged into a tree and was running off a car battery. The next day I resumed my travels and arrived at a "cross road." It was actually a place where two dirt tracks converged. My well-planned itinerary had me taking the better-travelled left route to the northwest.

To this day, I don't know what made me unexpectedly turn right. All I know is that I felt an almost irresistible tug in that direction. My machine's handlebar seemed to swing of its own accord as I leaned into the turn and found myself heading along a rutted track leading I knew not exactly where.

That afternoon I came across a stranded white Ford sedan containing a couple and their two young children. They had been there for two days and were hungry, tired and frightened. Not too many people came along that northeast road. After poking around under the hood, I discovered that their fuel pump had failed. Using a piece of rubber I cut from their spare tire's inner tube, I was able to replace the torn diaphragm of the pump. They called me their angel which made me blush. Then they gratefully went on their way.

On July 21st, 1969, God used me as His messenger. The people I helped thought of me as a human angel. The terminology doesn't make much difference does it?

> *For He will send His angels for you,*
> *to guard you in all your paths.*
> (Psalms 91:11)

May this always be true for you.

42

MORE BANG FOR YOUR MINUTE

What new door opens when I complete
this item on my task list?

D o you struggle to fit everything you need to do into your day? High achieving individuals understand the importance of time management. If you are trying to increase your productivity, you need to develop time management skills.

As God's guidebook to life, the Bible offers advice on this subject. This wisdom is revealed through a Hebrew word that means, "and he awoke."

To get a clear understanding of this, let's look at the following two verses.

> ...She (Delilah) said, 'The Philistines are upon you,
> Samson,' and he awoke from his sleep...
> (Judges 16: 14)

> She said, 'The Philistines are upon you, Samson,'
> and he awoke from his sleep...
> (Judges 16:20)

The verses seem to say the same thing, don't they? This is why I say, "Everyone needs a rabbi." There is valuable information embedded beneath the surface. In the first verse, the word for 'and he awoke' (*VaYiKaTZ*) is spelled with five Hebrew letters and looks like this:

וייקץ

In verse 20, only four of the letters are used.

ויקץ

As you can see, in the second example one of the little letters, called a *Yud*, is missing. If you don't read Hebrew, simply treat the letters as shapes and you will see the contrast. What is the difference between words in each of the two verses?

Ancient Jewish wisdom emphasizes that whenever there is an extra appearance of that specific letter, *Yud*, it connotes a dose of God's spiritual power.

Looking at the verses in context we see that initially Samson possessed his unique, God-given strength. He could prevail over his enemies. By the second verse, Delilah has ordered his hair cut in contradiction to God's command and Samson has lost his power. In Samson's case, the missing letter lets us know that this isn't a simple awakening; his entire reality has shifted for the worse.

By comparison, when Jacob awakens in Genesis 28:16, the word *VaYiKaTZ* is spelled with two yuds. When he lay down to sleep, he did so as a fugitive, fleeing his brother Esau's wrath. However, while he slept God spoke to him. When Jacob awoke he was a man with a destiny. His reality had expanded.

Sometimes we end our sleep reluctantly and rub our eyes wondering what to do. That is an awaken with only one *yud*. Far better to leap out of bed filled with resolve and excitement at tasks to be undertaken. Sleep isn't an escape from life, but rather a necessary rejuvenating step for facing a new day with new opportunities.

What is the time management lesson that we can all use? One important tool of time management is a task list. (Tip: Have only one task list and keep it in one place.) However, there is a difference between tasks that are complete in themselves and those that are stepping stones.

That difference relates to our perception, not to the job. For instance, we can look at, "Finish July sales spreadsheet" as the end of that particular project, or it can lead towards behaving more productively in the future. Preparing a meal can be a job in itself which ends when the food is ready, or it can be a step on the way towards spending valuable time eating as a family and keeping physically and spiritually healthy.

In life, we grow and achieve more from tasks whose completion opens the door to grander achievements.

Similarly, in our time management, we can always ask "What then?" What new door does completing this item on my task list, even if it is sleep, allow me to do? When tasks on our list relate to a greater goal, in sync with God's wishes, we tackle them more enthusiastically and more efficiently. Each day has the same 24 hours. How we approach them changes the quality of our life.

43

HENRY'S AWFUL MISTAKE

**The first steps towards fixing a problem
often make it worse.
Don't give up!**

In one of my children's favorite picture books, *Henry's
Awful Mistake*, Henry the duck decides to get rid of an
ant in his kitchen. Before long, his overly vigorous efforts
lead to a burst water pipe, a flooded house and evacuation.
You get the idea, right? When attempting to fix a problem,
one often finds that it has escalated into something much
more. You might wish you had left well alone.

Isn't that true in real life as well? You visit your dentist for a
minor tooth ache. He tells you that you need a root canal.
Soon you feel real pain. You wish you had just continued
living with the trivial tooth ache. But the mature part of you
knows that ignoring the problem wasn't a solution. The
temporary discomfort will lead to long term benefit.

Brad heard my lecture on how husbands and wives must
build one another up in front of their children. I urged wives
to ensure that their children stopped whatever they were doing
and went to the door to greet dad when he came home.

Brad told me that his children were frequently watching

television when he walked through the door. He determined to bring about major changes in his family.

"Brad," I said to him, "If you try to fix this problem, be sure that you can withstand the firestorm that your efforts will precipitate. The initial impact of most repair attempts is to make things much worse. One has to weather the storm and gently but firmly press for change. If, in the face of resistance one retreats, the situation becomes far worse than it was to begin with."

Brad assured me that he wouldn't give up. I wish I could report to you that Brad succeeded. Sadly, he did not. Perhaps over the years Brad had lost the ability to father with forceful conviction. Perhaps he and his wife weren't on the same page. But he now had a bigger problem than children who were indifferent to their father. He now had sullen children who resented him, and Brad blinked.

The angry reaction of his children knocked all the fight out of him. "I know that by starting this and giving up I have made things much worse," said Brad.

This principle of ancient Jewish wisdom is taught in the fifth chapter of Exodus. Remember that no part of Scripture is there merely for narrative. Every verse is part of the moral message to mankind. Every word is part of the guide to how the world really works.

After hundreds of years in slavery, the Israelites are accustomed to slavery as their normal condition. Now, God sends Moses to tell Pharaoh:

> *The Lord God of Israel said, 'Send out my people*
> *so they can celebrate for me in the desert.'*
>
> (Exodus 5:1)

Pharaoh reacts with fury. "Who is this God that I should listen to his voice?" He immediately worsens the lives of the Israelites with a frightful decree. They will no longer be supplied with the raw materials of production, yet their output must increase.

> *And now, get to work. You will not be given straw*
> *but you will deliver your quota of bricks.*
> (Exodus 5:18)

Not surprisingly, the Israelites hurl abuse at Moses. They are angry that he started up with Pharaoh causing this terrible worsening of their lives. Moses plaintively prays to God, "Ever since I came to Pharaoh to speak in Your name, he has done worse to this people." ˙

Here we learn that timeless truth. When you tamper with a status quo, no matter how bad it is, the odds are you are going to make it worse. However, if you stick with it, redemption will follow in the end, just as it eventually did for the Israelites.

Thus, whether you are grappling with an unsatisfactory family situation, a work-related dilemma, or perhaps a health matter, ancient Jewish wisdom offers three steps. One, make sure your goal is worthwhile enough to justify the fight. Two, set a plan for achieving the goal. Three, don't give up just because things seem to be getting worse. After all, you don't want to end up like Henry the duck who, after countless troubles, moved into a new house still accompanied by the original pesky ant.

WHAT DOESN'T BELONG?

**We all develop habits. Some handicap our lives
and diminish happiness.**

Here's a quick quiz: (answers below)

1. What does not belong in this list?

> oven, pot, toothbrush, ladle

2. What is the next term in this series?

> 1, 2, 3, 5, 8, 13, __

3. Fill in the blank:

> Atlanta, Everett, Ithaca, _____, Upland

Questions like these are used for measuring intelligence in
those notorious I.Q. tests. What do these types of questions
have in common? They ask you to identify patterns. The
ability to identify patterns is a mark of intelligence.

It is both intelligent and courageous to recognize repeated
patterns of destructive behavior. We all develop habits.
Some are positive, but others handicap our lives and diminish
happiness.

Think of men who marry unwisely, divorce and then marry someone strikingly similar to wife number one. Perhaps you know individuals whose temper has cost them jobs and relationships. Yet rather than identifying the problem they blame bad luck or other people for their failures. A deeply embedded destructive pattern can be as much of an addiction as alcohol or drugs.

Employ brutal honesty, searing focus and a wise mentor to search for harmful patterns in your own life. Keep searching – they're there. Once you know them, the battle to extirpate them can begin.

With its structure of countless subtle patterns, Scripture is an incomparable training ground for sharpening intelligence. It is not surprising that America's earliest universities were founded as Biblically-based institutes of learning.

For instance, have you noticed that both Joseph and David:

1) are younger siblings

2) are shepherds

3) are sent by father to visit older brothers (*Genesis 37:14 & I Samuel 17:17*)

4) are greeted by older brothers with anger (*Genesis 37:19 & I Samuel 17:28*)

5) are embraced by a king, made powerful and given a wife

6) are the only men in all Scripture described in Hebrew as NaVoN – insightful(*Genesis 41:39 & I Samuel 16:18*)

7) are the only men in all Scripture described in Hebrew as Yefei Mareh – good looking (*Genesis 39:6 & I Samuel 17:42*)

These are some of the many links between the lives of Joseph and David. For them to be a meaningless coincidence is very unlikely. Ancient Jewish wisdom reveals that the similarities are there to be observed and studied.

Indeed, David and Joseph seem to share a destiny. Joseph set up the nation of Israel in Egypt thereby creating a blueprint for Judaism in the Diaspora which applies with uncanny precision till today. David set up the nation of Israel in its homeland thereby creating a blueprint for Jewish habitation of Israel valid until today.

Furthermore, each is destined to play a role on that great day of God's choosing. A messianic descendant of Joseph will lay the groundwork for a messianic descendant of David.

However that discussion lies outside the scope of this Thought Tool. My focus here is that we recognize the importance of not living as victims of our genes, heritage, experiences and past choices, but realize that from today forward we are responsible for shaping our own lives. Each and every one of us can identify patterns in ourselves that with courage, determination and prayer can be modified, thereby transforming our lives. Discerning patterns will help us do that.

Answers:
1. *Toothbrush (the others relate to the kitchen)*
2. *21 (add the preceding two numbers to get the new one)*
3. *Oakland, Oceanside, Oklahoma City... (all are cities whose first letter begins with the next vowel)*

45

NEXT!

Treating people as numbers diminishes
the uniqueness that makes each special.

Although it is finally my turn I feel no delight when, without even glancing up, the post office clerk yells out "Next!" I understand that she has experienced a tiring day, maybe even a frustrating one, but her strident summons dehumanizes me. I feel as if my identity has been stripped away and I am now just another item being mechanically processed in numerical order. That's right; I have become just a number. Take a ticket. Next!

Turning a unique human being into an impersonal number can induce psychic disintegration. This is why the Nazis, in their evil twisted genius, tattooed a number onto the arms of their concentration camp victims. Though not in the same way, most militaries need to give new recruits identification numbers for organizational purposes, but to its great credit, the United States military places upon each soldier's uniform, his name not his number.

These reflections while waiting at the post office helped me understand in a deep, visceral way why God reacted so angrily when King David counted the people of Israel as described in the last chapter of the book of Samuel.

> *...and David's heart troubled him after he
> had counted the people and he said to God,
> 'I have sinned greatly in what I have done...'*
>
> (II Samuel 24:10)

Counting people, treating them as numbers, diminishes the uniqueness that makes each special. This would explain God's displeasure at King David diminishing the people of Israel by counting them. But wait just one moment....How about these verses?

> *...and God spoke to Moses saying, 'When you
> count the heads of the Children of Israel
> according to their number...'*
>
> (Exodus 30:11-12)

> *...and God spoke to Moses in the Sinai Desert in the
> Tent of Time....saying, 'Count the heads of
> the entire congregation of Israel...'*
>
> (Numbers 1:1-2)

This seems to suggest that when Moses performs a census all is well but when King David does the same thing, God punished him. He died shortly thereafter, at the beginning of the book of Kings.

The insight from ancient Jewish wisdom's interpretation of these events can profoundly help our own interactions and greatly enhance our ability to nurture friendships, romances and yes, business relationships.

When King David counted Israel, it was for no special purpose other than the satisfaction of a ruler knowing how many people he ruled. David did wrong because this needless counting turned them into numbers and dehumanized God's people.

When Moses counted the people in Exodus, it was in preparation for constructing the Tabernacle. In fact, one could say that the count built the tabernacle because the census was done by each person donating a silver coin. Rather than counting people, they counted these coins and then donated the silver to the holy construction project.

When Moses counted the people again, it was in preparation for designing the encampments they would inhabit for forty years. Counting people for a specific purpose is different. It can be uplifting to know that you are part of a group that is preparing for a special mission.

The valuable insight that escalates these Biblical stories into life-affirming strategies is that we are advised to treat all friends and even random acquaintances as unique and irreplaceable. It is so easy to fall into the habit of using exactly the same greeting such as "Hi" or "Hello" for everyone we know. It is easy to ignore people's names and address them as "dude," "buddy" or "girlfriend."

Part of God's Sinai message to mankind revolves around the idea of making our relationships with all the people in our lives each as distinctive as our relationship with God. That is one of the lessons of the commandments being given on two, parallel tablets. Studying this can help one make sure that each person with whom one interacts during the day feels that at that moment, he or she is the most important person in one's life.

Realistically, of course, I did not expect the person behind the post office counter to address me by name. But after I noted the clerk's lapel badge, when my turn finally came up, I smiled and said, "Hi, Annie, how you doing today?" I was pleased to hear her greet the person after me in line with a smile and the words, "Ma'am, I'm ready for you now." I kept on smiling.

46

BETRAYED BY A WORD

Never confuse what you want to hear with what the other person is actually saying.

Sandi had been dating Matt for a few months when she came to see me. They enjoyed one another's company and seemed to share common goals and beliefs. All the signs pointed to a shared future.

That is, until the Sunday that she and Matt attended a barbecue hosted by a group of his college friends. This was her first introduction to the group and she felt that she fitted in well. What surprised and troubled her was how Matt avoided giving any indication that they had a special relationship when introducing her. She might as well have been a random neighbor.

Sandi couldn't decide whether she was making a mountain out of a molehill or whether she had discovered a real problem in their relationship.

I opened a Bible and showed her how Genesis 24:2-8 details the instructions that Abraham directed to his servant, Eliezer, upon sending him to bring back a wife for Isaac. As the story unfolds, the Bible spends valuable ink having Eliezer repeat the entire conversation to Rebecca's family, including the instructions he had been given. (*Genesis 24:37-42*) Why didn't the Bible simply say, "And Eliezer told them all that his master had instructed"?

Ancient Jewish wisdom explains that any repetition in the Bible is there for a purpose. Indeed there are important variations between the story as it happened and as Eliezer recounts it. Let's analyze just one of those deviations.

Abraham said:

> *...don't take a wife for my son from the daughters of the Canaanites, <u>among whom I dwell</u>.*
> (Genesis 24: 3)

Eliezer said:

> *(My master told me)... 'Don't take a wife for my son from the daughters of the Canaanites <u>in whose land I dwell.</u>'*
> (Genesis 24:37)

Abraham fully believed God's word that the land was promised to him and already visualized it at his land (among whom I dwell, but in my land). Eliezer couldn't see beyond the readily evident. For him, it was the Canaanite's land (in whose land I dwell).

On the surface, the two statements are similar. In reality, they reflect a huge disparity between the two men. One was a visionary; the other a follower.

My advice to Sandi was that while she shouldn't end her friendship with Matt based just on what she had heard, she was wise to pay close attention to small details. People do reveal their inner thoughts by the words they use. I suggested raising the topic in a non-confrontational manner. Possibly Matt felt a word like "girlfriend" would trivialize their relationship and he didn't know what else to say. Or perhaps they were indeed on different pages.

When things go wrong in our romantic or family lives, or in our business or community interactions, we frequently say, "I should have seen it coming." Often we are so busy and distracted that we miss the warning flags. Then we cry, "What was I thinking?"

Most people, like Eliezer; inadvertently reveal themselves with their words. The trick is learning to listen well. Never confuse what you want to hear with what the other person is actually saying. In personal relationships and in business, words are a clue into the human soul; it is foolish to minimize their importance.

And Sandi? It turned out that Matt had given her many verbal clues indicating that marriage was far from his mind. She ended that relationship. A wedding invitation recently arrived from Sandi and Joe.

47

GO FOR IT

**Unlike the gods of Greek mythology,
God's directives aren't capricious.**

Encountering a stranger who knows more about your life than he should is eerie. Well, I don't mean to startle you, but I do know a private fact about you. I know that you are weighing up a decision in your life.

To be sure, I do not know any details. I have no idea whether you are considering a geographic move, a job change, an investment, or whether you are considering a family or medical decision, but there is certainly some fork in the road that you are confronting. And because I am quite ignorant of your particular situation, I am unable to advise any specifics.

However, I can help you focus some ancient Jewish wisdom onto your predicament. This will help illuminate your direction just as focusing a flashlight in a dark forest at night reveals previously unseen paths.

Let's start with the very first Biblical indication that Abraham is someone special. It is the life-challenge described in this verse:

And God said to Abram, 'Go for yourself out of
your country and from your birthplace...'
(Genesis 12:1)

This new directive sets Abraham's life on course.

This is the first in a succession of challenges throughout Abraham's life. His final life-challenge is the sacrifice of Isaac.

Take your son, your only son, whom you love, Isaac,
and go for yourself to the land of Moriah ...
(Genesis 22:2)

I want you to observe that both Abraham's first challenge and his final challenge are presented in terms of, "Go for yourself."

In the Lord's language, that recurring phrase of two Hebrew words, pronounced as LeCH LeCHa, looks like this:

לֶךְ   לְךָ
for yourself   go

Though pronounced slightly differently, you can see that the two Hebrew words "Go" and "For Yourself" are actually one and the same.

What a brilliantly incandescent insight! God is saying to Abraham, "Whatever I command you to do, every challenge I lay in your path, step forward to meet it FOR YOUR OWN BENEFIT. Do not do it just to please me – know that there is also value in it for you." Unlike the gods of Greek mythology, God's directives aren't capricious.

Back now to whatever crossroads you are confronting. We

know that God does not always indicate to us the path He wants us to take. Our Heavenly Father often stands back, granting us the privilege of making our own choices just as parents train a child to make its own decisions.

Clearly, whenever a forthcoming decision torments us it is one of those occasions when the good Lord is encouraging us to grow. We should embrace the challenge promptly.

The lesson of one word meaning both "Go" and "For Yourself", is that generally, making a decision is better than procrastination. Obviously, I'm not talking about reckless, impulsive or rebellious choices. But if you are acting maturely, in good faith, a wrong decision is usually better than no decision.

Boaters like me know that when you're stationary, your rudder is useless. You have no control. Moving in the wrong direction is better than not moving, because you have momentum to correct course.

Here are three steps to overcome inertia. Start by analyzing the pros and cons of each choice. Then, absorb the emotional imperative to step off the high diving board. After all, no one would get married, have children or start a business if they required an ironclad guarantee of success. Finally, deploy your power of faith to step forward. There is genuine joy in confronting decisions. We should stride forth with a debonair smile on our face and calm confidence in our hearts.

Lech Lech – Go for yourself. Take that step forward. Make that decision now! It is for you.

48

RETREAT TO ADVANCE

**Human creativity thrives in an environment of
thrust, retreat and then thrust again.**

Have you ever experienced intense frustration trying to
recall something?

Perhaps it is the name of someone you want to call. Sometimes it is a tune that is dancing around your mind just
out of memory's reach. There was an item that my wife
asked me to pick up at the store. "Write it down so you'll
remember," she said. "Not necessary," I replied. And there
I was wandering the aisles hoping I would see something
that might jog my memory.

You scrunch up your brow; rub your temples with your
fists and contort your face into a bizarre mask of concentration. None of this helps. Finally, a disconnected thought
pops into your mind or you run into an acquaintance and
stop to chat. A few minutes later you remember whatever
it was that was tormenting you.

Isn't it amazing? All that sweating and stressing to remember
and – nothing! Then three minutes of doing something else,
and bingo! There it is. It came back to you as clearly as could be.

Like all of us, I spend my day tackling challenges. Sometimes there's a problem baffling me. Then I put it out of mind and retire for the night. Often in the early pre-dawn hours I will awaken and am instantly aware that I have had a creative thought breakthrough. Grabbing the pen and pad I always keep alongside my bed and which I recommend as a vital business tool, I can hurriedly scrawl down the answer to the daunting problem from the day before.

Every time this happens I am amazed, yet it shouldn't astound me. After all, this is one of those timeless truths of ancient Jewish wisdom. Human creativity thrives in an environment of thrust, retreat and then thrust again. Work the problem, back off and then return to the problem. It will yield more rapidly than it would in one long protracted push.

This is the principle of both sleep and the Sabbath.

Withdrawing from economic and other forceful interactions with the world during the Sabbath doesn't lessen our productivity; it enhances it. Six days of creativity depend for their effectiveness upon the one day of rest and retreat.

The function of sleep itself is one of the 125 greatest mysteries of science, according to *Science* magazine. It certainly appears that any creature that managed to do away with sleep would enjoy enormous evolutionary advantage. First of all it would have no extended period of vulnerability to predators. Second, it would have significantly more time available for food gathering and reproduction. Yet we all need sleep. Trying to override this need with stimulants doesn't work long term.

This is a physical parallel to a spiritual reality. Just as our bodies require sleep, so do our minds and souls. Creativity and productivity are enhanced by regular periods of withdrawal.

Life is full of stressful problems. We think we can't afford to stop running. Sometimes we think we can't even take the time to talk to God on a daily basis. Yet if we force ourselves to retreat, we will find that we are using time more efficiently, not less.

In addition to setting times for sleep, prayer and the Sabbath, I think it's a good idea to make a regular appointment with yourself right in your calendar just as you make appointments to meet with a customer or client. Mark it down as thinking time. It might only be twenty minutes of intense concentration on a problem. Work at that problem keeping extraneous ideas out of your head. Then switch your focus to something else. Let your subconscious work the problem for you.

When God set up the rhythms of night and day, six days of work and the Sabbath, He was providing the means by which individuals and societies thrive. We only prosper when we follow those rhythms rather than fight them. Oh yes, writing down a shopping list doesn't hurt either.

49

FEELING LUCKY, PUNK?

**While God's hand is all-powerful,
we need to guide our choices
in the correct direction.**

I misquote. In his 1971 classic, *Dirty Harry*, Clint Eastwood actually said,

> *"You've got to ask yourself one question:
> 'Do I feel lucky?' Well, do ya punk?"*

How about you? When things seem to be going your way, from finding a new job to meeting a potential mate do you marvel at your luck? When you lose a job or friend, do you rail at it instead?

Let's look at three seemingly lucky men and one unlucky one, from the Bible.

1) Abraham's servant, Eliezer, is sent on a mission to find a wife for Abraham's son, Isaac. Entrusted with this momentous errand, Eliezer devises a strategy. He will ask for a drink of water at the well, and if the girl offers water not only to him, but also to his camels, he will know that she is Isaac's future wife. How lucky for posterity that Rebecca fit the bill. (Genesis 24)

2) Caleb promises that whoever leads the Israelites to victory against the town of Kiryat Sefer will marry his daughter. It turns out to be the Godly and valiant Otniel. (Joshua 15)

3) Confronted by the terrifying Goliath, King Saul proclaims that whoever defeats the giant will marry his daughter. How lucky that David is not only a great warrior but also a great man. (I Samuel 17)

4) Jephthah (more accurately pronounced Yiftach) swears that if God leads him to victory against the Amonites, he will sacrifice whatever first comes out of his house to greet him upon his return. Unfortunately, his daughter is first and tragedy ensues. (Judges 11)

All four stories describe someone who appears to be leaving important decisions to random luck. Can you see a reason why the first three stories worked out well, while poor Jephthah's didn't?

The answer is that only Jephthah left things to chance. Each of the first three accounts involved a test of character. That is far from blind luck.

Imagine a friend handing you a small ball and directing you to use it to knock down a tower of blocks at the far end of the room. He thinks he's given you an almost impossible task. But you decide not to entrust the outcome to a lucky throw.

Instead of tossing the ball, you drop it down a chute, where it gathers speed. At the bottom, it strikes the door latch of a small cage releasing a hamster that scuttles up a ramp to a tempting morsel of food. (Remember those goofy Rube Goldberg contraptions?)

The ramp is really a see-saw and the hamster's weight causes it to drop and hit an electric switch which starts a model train rumbling down a miniature track and so on.

Eventually the final ridiculous act in this multi-part mechanical comedy triggers a device which knocks down the stack of wooden building blocks.

We sometimes leave things to luck when with effort we can improve our odds. Eliezer, Caleb and Saul knew that invisible links connect courage and compassion to the characteristics of a good spouse. While God would oversee the final outcome, they were stipulating a meaningful test. (Don't try this one at home)

Jephthah's condition was meaningless.

Part of improving our lives every day is leaving as little as possible to chance. Life is full of invisible links and marvelous devices that can convert our actions into positive results. While God's hand is all-powerful, we need to guide our choices in the correct direction as much as we can. He rewards our focus and purpose.

I am gratified that thousands have followed the principles I teach to help them move from Jephthah like randomness to the success that follows deliberate behavior.

Clint Eastwood may have left things to chance, but we do better by remembering that life rarely resembles the movies.

HOW TO BE A WISEGUY

In wealth creation and successful family life, wisdom is far more important than intelligence.

Ninety years ago, in June, 1919, World War I officially ended with the signing of the Treaty of Versailles. French field marshal, Ferdinand Foch, famously said,

"This is not Peace. It is an Armistice for twenty years."

He was out by three months! By September, 1939, France was again at war with Germany.

A year earlier, in September, 1938, British Prime Minister Neville Chamberlain returned from meeting with Adolf Hitler in Munich saying,

"...a British Prime Minister has returned from Germany bringing peace with honor. I believe it is peace for our time."

Only one year later German bullets were killing British boys.

Prime Minister Chamberlain was undeniably an intelligent man. He had done far better in school and university than had Winston Churchill, yet it was Churchill who in the early 1930s knew that war with Germany was inevitable.

In politics, as in wealth creation and successful family life, wisdom is far more important than intelligence. This is great news because there is not much we can do to increase our intelligence, but we can certainly increase our wisdom.

Intelligence governs how quickly one tackles abstract ideas and how rapidly one assimilates and processes data. Doing this well is certainly helpful in many professions, but it only goes so far. Being wise means knowing how the world really works. Intelligence is largely hereditary while wisdom can be gained. I would like to impart to you the first three steps in gaining wisdom.

The first step is getting to know God.

> *The beginning of wisdom is fear of God.*
> (Psalms 111:10)

Wisdom can be a powerful tool for both good and evil. Many people are motivated by their understanding of God's wishes. Others act in ways intended to defy God. Much of life revolves around spiritual factors like love, trust, faith, optimism and courage. Without an understanding of this spiritual side of life it is difficult to function effectively in the real world.

The second step in gaining wisdom is to eschew fantasy and embrace fact. Read quality non-fiction and accustom yourself to accept people and circumstances as they are rather than as you'd like them to be. Reduce the amount of time you devote to amusement. The word 'amusement' means 'without thinking.' (a = without, as in amoral; and muse = think) Instead, set aside regular 'thinking-time' appointments with yourself. This not only helps to grow your wisdom, it also makes you happier.

The third step, and yes I know this is very difficult, is to work on suppressing one's emotions while trying to analyze a situation. Let me show you where the Bible elegantly demonstrates this point.

When Queen Esther invited Haman and the king to a banquet in her chambers (Esther 5:4), this prestigious invitation boosted Haman onto an emotional high. In his elated mood, being spurned by his nemesis, Mordechai, infuriated him. When he consulted with his friends (in the Hebrew, OHaVaV, which means 'those who loved him') and his wife (Esther 5:10) they giddily embraced both Haman's euphoria and anger, advising him to hang Mordechai.

Shortly thereafter, Haman was humiliated by the king (Esther 6:10) and he again consulted his wife and friends (again, in the Hebrew text 'those who loved him') about this apparent reversal of his fortunes.

> *And Haman told his wife, Zeresh, <u>and those who loved him</u>, all that had happened, and his <u>wise advisors</u> and Zeresh his wife said to him..*
> (Esther 6:13)

Abandoning their emotional connection to Haman transforms his sycophantic lovers into wise advisors. They clinically examine the situation and with wisdom recognize the bad news that his star is descending (Esther 6:13).

Though you cannot increase your Intelligence Quotient, you can increase your Wisdom Quotient. I hope these three steps help you on your path.

THOUGHT TOOL
51

PATHWAYS TO PROSPERITY

**Bible holydays are not random events
scattered around the calendar**

Bible festivals were never merely holidays to the Jews —
they are holydays. What's the difference? Well, a vacation or a holiday might just mean that you don't have to
go to work or follow your normal routine. On a holyday
you *get* to do things, very special things that polish your
personality, sculpt your soul, and redirect your life.

Furthermore, Bible holydays are not random events scattered
around the calendar. They are exquisitely positioned high-
lights in the tapestry of time. Each holyday is linked, not only
to the beating heart of a living nation but also to every other
holyday in a synchronized system of spiritual development.

Take for instance the holyday of Shavuot, widely known
as Pentecost.

This holyday is bound up with Passover, celebrated seven
weeks earlier. Starting on Passover, there is a formal count
which marks the march of the forty-nine days connecting the two holydays. Picture a child's board game where
you need to visit forty-nine steps from when you leave the
START box until you arrive at the FINISH mark.

The holyday pathway starts with Passover, chiefly characterized by the eating of unleavened crackers known in Hebrew as matzo or LeCHeM ONI. The word LeCHeM means bread, while ONI possesses several meanings but the one of interest to us here is "poverty."

Thus, the Torah instructs that on Passover,

> *...seven days shall you eat matzo...*
> *the bread of poverty...*
> (Deuteronomy 16:3)

The pathway ends with Shavuot or Pentecost (from the Greek for 50 referring to Shavuot being the fiftieth day from Passover) celebrated with real bread, as described in Leviticus 23:15-20. Ancient Jewish wisdom explains that while unleavened bread or matzo is rightly described as the bread of poverty, it is regular bread which is known as the bread of prosperity.

This idea that bread is linked to prosperity lies at the root of such colloquialisms as "Can you lend me some bread?" or "Do you have any dough?" Yes, bread means money. When someone has enough bread to eat, he is making a living.

Ancient Jewish wisdom teaches that in the reality of God's world, time and place do not exist independently but only as an interchangeable amalgam. As the twentieth century dawned, western physics began to catch on and relativity was born. The time-space continuum was on everyone's lips.

In popular parlance people began to say things like "I just wasn't in a good place," when referring to a bad time in their lives. What they really meant was "I just wasn't in a good time," but since time and place are interchangeable, all is well.

Thus our pathway leading from a time called Passover to another time called Shavuot, forty-nine days away, could be accurately viewed as a pathway from a place called Passover to a place called Shavuot, forty-nine steps away.

Or, more helpfully, we could visualize these two Biblical holydays as a journey down a pathway from a place of poverty (bread of poverty) to a place of prosperity (bread of prosperity).

It now becomes rather important to understand the nature of this pathway that can take us from a place/time of poverty – Passover, to a place/time of prosperity – Shavuot. Could this pathway have clues for anyone, anywhere, anytime who is trying to walk the path of prosperity?

The answer, happily, is yes. Ancient Jewish wisdom reveals that one vital emphasis of this forty-nine step pathway is care and consideration of our relationships with our friends. During this forty-nine day period we focus on a famous instance in Jewish history when there was serious negligence about the nurturing of friendships. The result was the shattering of twelve thousand important relationships, leading to the deaths of those involved.

One of the life-enhancing messages of the time between these two holydays now becomes clear. Our relationships are our road to prosperity. People tend to hire, they tend to buy from, and they tend to do business with individuals whom they know, like, and trust. If few other humans know you, like you, and trust you, you might well end up with very little bread. We don't make friends in order to get wealthy; but people without friends rarely attain wealth. It is a huge mistake to think that somewhere down the road, once we have built our careers, we will have time to cherish our special friendships and show our friends how much they mean to us. Without those relationships and friendships with others, we won't even be on the right path.

THOUGHT TOOL

52

WHAT'S IN YOUR TOOLBOX?

Do I really need a wrench
that will last forever?

I enjoy owning and using tools. I profoundly enjoy owning and using high quality tools to build and fix things. Hardly ever do I purchase tools without the lifetime guarantee offered by outstanding brands like Craftsman or Snap-on. Yes, they do cost much more than those no-name-brand tools out there, but my wife never questions the cost difference. She knows that great tools are, well, a guy sort of thing.

But wait! Do I really need a wrench that will last forever? Would I really find it impossible to repair the closet hinge with a screwdriver that will only last for another six years? Why should I care if my nineteen-dollar-drill does a great job for me today but will be a rusty relic by next year?

Actually it does make a difference. For me there is value in handling a tool that was built so well that my grandchildren will one day be able to use it. What is that value? Using high quality tool imparts these three benefits:

1. **Confidence:** I can apply full force to that wrench confident that it won't bend and propel me headlong into the engine compartment of my boat.

2. **Continuity:** I didn't purchase that screwdriver, my father did. In using it, I am not only repairing the closet door I am a living link in the chain of my family's tradition of masculine mechanical competence.

3. **Character:** I am no dabbling dilettante. I am a professional using professional tools with a professional's sense of purpose about my work.

In the same way I ask myself whether there is really any value in designing my life and regulating it in accordance with a Biblical world-view. After all, do I really need a tool that has been around for 3,000 years? Would it really be problematic to make life decisions guided by the latest fads and trends that will be scorned and forgotten in five years time? Why should I care if secularism's latest foolish fashion shapes my thinking today? I can always get a new foolish fashion tomorrow quite inexpensively.

Actually, yes, we do need a tool that has been around for a long time and will continue to be around for a long time. Sculpting my life, family and business to the shape of Biblical reality confers great benefits.

1. **Confidence:** I can push ahead through life's challenges with full force and with all my will, knowing that the ideas on which I am relying have endured through time.

2. **Continuity:** I am not only living my life, raising my family and building my economic reality but I am also a living link in the chain that stretches from Sinai to the bright shining Tomorrow.

3. **Character:** Instead of merely meandering through life,

I have a professional sense of purpose. All I do is imbued with my role of bringing God's will alive.

The wealth created by the west, the art and culture, even the very manners practiced by a civil society are all products of Biblical ideas. Successful nations have emulated those traditions. That is why buses, banks and bathrooms even in such far off places like Beijing and Bangkok, now look pretty much like those in western Biblically-founded cultures like Brussels and Boston. This powerful system of organizing life that has done so much for societies and cultures can do the same for our lives and our families.

I hope this collection of Thought Tools will help you forge the link between the Biblical foundations of the past and the bright vitality of your life. The more that things change, the more we need to depend upon those things that never change. Reminding you what those permanent principles are is one of the reasons we produced this book.

THE WAY TO PEACE AND TRANQUILITY

Shalom

שׁ ל מ

Shortly before he died in 1981, Nobel Prize winning scientist, Max Delbruck, delivered a lecture at Cal Tech which I was privileged to attend. He spoke engagingly about having encountered the already famous Albert Einstein in one of the elevators of the Planck Institute in Berlin before World War Two.

The audience chuckled as he described how he almost wished for the cables to snap so he could watch Einstein cope with one of his gravity-themed thought-experiments suddenly turning terrifyingly practical. I found myself not only educated by the lecture, but also entertained. Delbruck peppered his technical analyses with quotations from poetry and allusions to music. Along with the rest of the audience, I was utterly charmed.

Returning home, I related the lecture to my wife as best as I could and told her of my reaction. Not since I had taken leave of the great teachers at my yeshiva had I encountered anyone who related to almost every aspect of the world as seamlessly as did Max Delbruck. With her style of simple directness that had intimidated me from the day we met, my bride wanted to know why I didn't call Delbruck and arrange a private meeting. Trying to explain to her why this was a terrible idea was quite difficult, so I obtained his phone number from a friend in Pasadena and placed the call.

To my astonishment, Dr. Delbruck himself answered the phone. He sounded amused when I described what it was about his speech that enchanted me and he graciously consented to see Susan and me. Our most undisturbed opportunity to talk, he explained, would be if we accompanied him on his weekly hike over the hills behind Pasadena.

The following Tuesday afternoon Susan and I met the distinguished scientist at his modest bungalow near the campus of the California Institute of Technology. As we looked around his library he recounted how the previous evening he had hosted a book club meeting at which he had reviewed a recent best-seller. That evening, he would be playing the violin for a chamber orchestra recital. We chatted for a while longer, then set off at a brisk clip up the rugged terrain. He climbed so swiftly that I began to fear that I would eventually have to carry the elderly man back to town. After an hour had elapsed, I changed my mind. It was quite clear that he would be carrying me.

The afternoon was unforgettable! We discussed history, biology, popular entertainment, chemistry, literature, geology, atomic physics, photography, politics, and genetics. To be perfectly honest, much of the conversation was not so much a discussion as it was Delbruck talking and Susan and me raptly listening.

"Do your students enjoy the same unbridled curiosity about every facet of the world as you do?" I asked him. He expressed deep concern and was uncharacteristically vehement when, with sad eyes, he assured me that nothing could be further from the truth. Most science students today, he contemptuously exclaimed, expressed almost no interest in anything outside their area of specialization, and knew even less. Then, in a prediction that I have come to believe to be increasingly true, he warned that this interdisciplinary illiteracy would eventually threaten American achievement.

Sadly, a few months later Max Delbruck was gone. But how the memories of that afternoon linger in my mind!

Interdisciplinary Literacy

In the years following that memorable afternoon, it became clear to me that most of the great minds of the past also saw no barriers isolating each of the many different ways of coming to know our wonderful world. An example is one of my heroes, Winston Churchill. What was he? Soldier, journalist, politician, painter, novelist, bricklayer, orator, or world leader? Perhaps he was the last only on account of the seamless unity of the first seven.

What a pleasure it would have been to have sat in on a sociable seventeenth century evening with these three friends: poet John Milton, architect Christopher Wren and scientist Robert Boyle. Not only did they happily get along with one another, but they were also comfortable and knowledgeable in each other's areas of expertise. Wren designed St Paul's cathedral in London, and was also a distinguished astronomer. Milton was a theologian, as was Boyle. The latter not only had a law of physics named for him, Boyles Law, but he also translated the Bible into many languages in his role as the head of the Society for Propagating the Gospel in New England.

Think of Leonard de Vinci, who was not only a painter and sculptor but also a designer of helicopters! Think of almost any truly great human being and you will find someone who simultaneously developed the many parts of his personality rather than focusing on only one narrow area to the detriment of the others.

Have you ever heard some cruel critic calling a computer enthusiast a geek or a nerd? The derision you hear in those words might result from this very point. Certain kinds of males seem to find computers to be all absorbing. (Very few females seem to fall victim to this particular form of fatal fascination.) These guys' technical obsessions leave them little time or energy for any other pursuits, so they occasionally strike us as psychically misshapen; almost like a dwarf with a tiny body and an enormous head. They are very obviously indifferent to almost anything nontechnical while being conspicuously advanced in the one narrow area of digital science.

I suspect that most of us are more comfortable interacting with people with broad interests, which may be why people with intense but narrow interests so often find themselves socially isolated.

Escape from Overspecialization

There is escape from this dreadful peril of over specialization, and it is part of the treasure found in the Lord's language.

The Hebrew word ShaLoM is the key to welcoming a well-rounded perspective into our lives. It has several meanings, and as always, the treasure lies beneath the layers of confusion that conceal how these several meanings really merge into one overarching principle.

These meanings are:

> Peace;
> Complete;
> Pay;
> Greetings.

Let us start unearthing the treasure by attempting to combine the first two meanings – peace and complete. Imagine my returning home one evening from work to find an unwashed vagrant, whom I have never seen before, camped on my living-room rug. He has unrolled a smelly sleeping bag and lit a fire in my fireplace. As I walk in the door, he insolently eyes me and lazily drawls, "Hi."

"Hi, yourself" I might say to him. "You have thirty seconds to get out of this house."

He careful completes the delicate operation of removing an unappetizing hot dog from the fire, before answering, "Stay cool, man. We both want peace, right? I'll keep to my half of the living room and you can have the other half."

Meanwhile I am having difficulty trying to decide whether I should resort to my baseball bat or to my twelve gauge shotgun. Sensing my thoughts, he again assures me that he only wants peace. "Let us sit down together and discuss a peaceful solution to our dilemma," he urges me.

This is a gross misunderstanding of the real meaning of peace. Peace is inseparable from its constituent element—completion or totality. I must be made complete or total before we can even begin discussing peace.

In this instance, that vagrant must leave my house and restore me to the condition in which I was before he interfered in my life. Only then can we discuss peace.

This example also happens to reveal how the third meaning, payment, fits in. If a customer takes a pair of shoes from the department store salesman, there is no completion and no peace -- just yet. She must first pay for those shoes. That way the store and its salesman are made complete or whole, and then peace can reign. Were she to walk out of the store without paying, there would be little peace. Instead there would be a charge of shoplifting and considerable turbulence for all involved. Peace is far preferable, but can only be attained by all parties achieving totality through payment. Not only does peace depend upon payment for things taken, but it has to be fair –a market value payment. This is the genius behind the Fifth Amendment to our great American constitution. In it we find the words, "nor shall private property be taken for public use without just compensation."

Our wise Founders clearly understood that peace depends upon just compensation. In fact, given the familiarity with

Hebrew that many of them enjoyed, it is likely that they also understood that peace and payment are the same word.

Obviously the fourth meaning – greetings – simply flows from the first three meanings: peace, totality, and payment. When I greet a new arrival or bid farewell to her by uttering the word, ShaLoM, I am expressing the hope that we shall both enjoy the full tranquility that can only come from totality and discharged obligations or payment.

And that is only the first jewel from the buried treasure chest.

The larger diamond lies just beneath the next shovel-full of sand. Again we must examine the first two meanings for SHaLoM -- peace and complete. The idea is that peace or tranquility can only come from...

Read more in the book

Buried Treasure:
**Secrets for Living
from the Lord's Language**

By Rabbi Daniel Lapin

Did you enjoy this book?

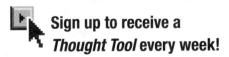 **Sign up to receive a**
Thought Tool every week!

Thought Tools is a free weekly email from Rabbi Daniel and Susan Lapin. This short message brings you spiritual tips, techniques, and knowledge that you can use to improve your life in four areas: family, faith, friends, and finances.

Regardless of your background, _Thought Tools_ offers you fascinating glimpses into the Lord's language – Hebrew, little-known secrets from Ancient Jewish Wisdom, information on Jewish holidays and customs, Bible secrets, and other mystical traditions with practical implications.

Expand your range of consciousness and spark conversation with family and friends by sharing these nuggets of wisdom.

Sign up for _Thought Tools_ at
www.rabbidaniellapin.com

"The more things change, the
more we depend on those things
that never change. That's why
you need a rabbi."
— Rabbi Daniel Lapin

TEACHINGS
FROM RABBI DANIEL LAPIN

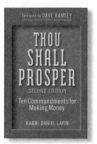

Thou Shall Prosper (2nd Edition)

Ten Commandments for Making Money

Thou Shall Prosper explains:
- Why Jews throughout the ages flourish economically
- How you can benefit from this Jewish wisdom
- What "being in business" means, whether you are a professional, a CEO or flipping burgers
- Why you should never retire

Buried Treasure

Secrets for Living from the Lord's Language

Buried Treasure gives you a glimpse into God's understanding of:
- Love
- Happiness
- Faith
- Wealth

Thought Tools 2008:

Fifty Timeless Truths to Uplift and Inspire

- Reprogram the software of your soul with these popular bite-sized messages
- Each page provides a launching pad for thoughtful conversation and growth
- Travel with Rabbi Lapin through the pages of the Bible, the Jewish year and the Hebrew language

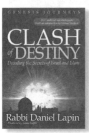

Two audio CD set plus
a 16-page study guide

Genesis Journeys: Clash of Destiny

Decoding the Secrets of Israel and Islam

- What Muslims know about prayer that most people, even those who pray regularly, don't
- The dark side of laughter
- Why recruits in Arab terrorist training camps say "Heil Hitler"
- How to rise above our cultural and genetic legacy

Two audio CD set plus
a 16-page study guide

Genesis Journeys: Tower of Power

Decoding the Secrets of Babel

- How every Hebrew Biblical name has a meaning that sheds light on the person's true character
- The seductive lure of socialism and how it affects you
- What both Abraham and Pharaoh have to do with the Tower of Babel
- Why companies often fail after constructing huge buildings

Two audio CD set plus
a 16-page study guide

Genesis Journeys: The Gathering Storm

Decoding the Secrets of Noah

- What parenting technique Noah used that resulted in his children being saved
- Why the dimensions given for the ark are vital for your life
- The hidden meaning of the entire "begat" section of Genesis
- Similarities between our own days and the days preceding the Flood

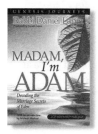

Genesis Journeys:
Madam, I'm Adam

Decoding the Marriage Secrets of Eden

- Why understanding the Hebrew words for man and woman can improve your marriage
- Can "being in the mood" destroy your marriage?
- What is the difference between a physically mature male and a Man?
- Who is more responsible when a couple divorces – the husband or the wife?

Two audio CD set plus a 16-page study guide

Biblical Blueprint Audio Series

One Audio CD

Boost Your Income

Three Spiritual Steps to Success

- Why Jews have flourished economically
- Do you treat money like candles or cake
- Money advice from Joseph and his brothers
- Do you make money or take money
- Should you do what you love or love what you do

One Audio CD

Day for Atonement

Heavenly Gift of Spiritual Serenity

Day for Atonement answers these questions:
- Are you handicapped by yesterday's mistakes
- The truth behind astrology and horoscopes
- Why the Bible mentions the Day of Atonement three separate times
- Jonah's lesson for your life

One Audio CD

The Ten Commandments

How Two Tablets Can Transform Your Life and Direct Our Nation

- Why the Ten Commandments must be displayed in public
- How positive human interaction is based on these vital verses
- Why they had to be on two tablets, not just one
- How crucial differences between America and the old Soviet Union are dictated by each country's attitude toward these phrases

One Audio CD

Let Me Go

How to Overcome Life's Challenges and Escape Your Own Egypt

- What three Bible secrets can help everyone escape difficult times
- Did Moses really say, "Let My People Go"
- How to recognize your angels in disguise
- Why the Jews needed to leave Egypt in broad daylight

One Audio CD

Festival of Lights

Transform Your 24/7 Existence Into a 25/8 Life

- Are you handicapped by how you think of time
- What do the numbers 8 and 25 mean in ancient Jewish wisdom
- What lessons of Chanuka are embedded in Scripture

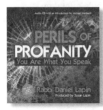

One Audio CD

Perils of Profanity

You Are What You Speak

- How vulgar speech damages your chances for success in both business and personal relationships
- Why Joseph recounted his dreams to his brothers, knowing that they would be angered
- What damage to the soul comes from using or hearing profanity
- Why everyone, even those who don't curse, should be concerned about the prevalence of foul language in our culture

ENDORSEMENTS
FOR RABBI DANIEL LAPIN

"Even those of us who invest our lives in teaching and advising other people need our own sources of wisdom and advice, in other words – a rabbi, and Daniel Lapin is my rabbi. His background and scholarship uniquely equip him to help people like me extract the deep meaning of each Biblical verse to improve every aspect of my life. And let me tell you, as someone who has been speaking to large audiences for years this rabbi can really entertain while he educates – you'll laugh while you learn. If you want access to a life-transforming Biblical blueprint for your life, make Daniel Lapin your rabbi – you won't regret it."

> Zig Ziglar, *author and nationally renowned motivational speaker*
> Texas

"Rabbi Daniel Lapin's lectures are entertaining, eloquent, and elegant. I enjoy the information he provides and the Talmudic perspective he brings."

> Dr. Marvin Olasky, *Editor-in-Chief*
> World Magazine
> University of Texas Professor

"How is it that this British accented Orthodox Rabbi has gained the attention and respect of so many leaders from all walks of life? It doesn't take long to know the answer once you have heard Rabbi Lapin speak. He possesses the rare combination of Biblical knowledge, and a compelling intellect coupled with down to earth wisdom and humor that leaves you truly the better for having listened."

> Rice Broocks, *Senior Pastor*
> Bethel World Outreach Center
> Nashville, Tennessee

"While many today give lip-service to 'the Judeo-Christian tradition,' I find Rabbi Daniel Lapin to be a true spokesman for it in our time. Like me, he believes that understanding Genesis is the foundation for a correct view of the world. That's why I am pleased to recommend his Genesis Journeys audio program."

Dr. D. James Kennedy, *Ph.D.* (1930-2007)
Coral Ridge Presbyterian Church

"For over a decade I have been watching my friend Rabbi Daniel Lapin's spell-binding oratory electrify large Christian audiences. His Biblical scholarship, love of America, and command of the English language bring the Bible to life. In a unique way he transforms ancient verses into effective solutions to our modern problems. Rabbi Lapin's insights and depth of knowledge make this a tremendous resource. This brand new audio program can now make America's rabbi part of your life just as he is part of mine."

Jay Alan Sekulow, *Chief Counsel*
American Center for Law and Justice

"Rabbi Daniel Lapin is an Orthodox rabbi who has joined me several times on our national and international television broadcasts. Rabbi Lapin presents the Bible in both entertaining and informative ways. He presents hidden nuggets of Bible truth in an exciting manner with laser beam intensity. You will enjoy Genesis Journeys in the growth and development of your spiritual life."

Dr. John C. Hagee,
Cornerstone Church
San Antonio, Texas